ENGLAND RUGBY

THE OFFICIAL YEARBOOK
2015/16

This edition published in 2015

Copyright © Carlton Books Limited 2015

Carlton Books Limited
20 Mortimer Street
London W1T 3JW

A CIP catalogue record for this book is available from the British
Library.

10 9 8 7 6 5 4 3 2 1

ISBN 978-1-78097-671-6

Project director: Martin Corteel
Project Art Editor: Luke Griffin
Author: Iain Spragg
Picture research: Paul Langan
Book designer: Darren Jordan
Editorial assistants: Chris Hawkes and David Ballheimer
Production: Maria Petalidou

Printed in Slovenia

England Rugby

ENGLAND RUGBY

THE OFFICIAL YEARBOOK
2015/16

CARLTON BOOKS

England Rugby's motto: "Hundreds before you. Thousands around you. Millions behind you." Players, such as Owen Farrell, read this uplifting message as they walk along the tunnel to the pitch at Twickenham.

Contents

England
Rugby

FOREWORD BY:

Stuart Lancaster

Hello and welcome to the 2015 edition of the official England Rugby Yearbook. It's been another hugely exciting few months of international rugby for England sides at all levels and on behalf of them all, I'd like to thank you, the fans, for your incredible support.

The 2015 RBS 6 Nations was an incredible tournament and although it was tough to beat France at Twickenham on the final weekend but still miss out on the title, I was incredibly proud of the way the team performed that day and throughout the Championship.

I'd like to congratulate the Under 20 team coached by Jon Callard after they backed up their success at the Junior World Championship last year by winning their Six Nations title and the England men's and women's Sevens sides, who both ensured Great Britain will be represented at the Rio de Janeiro 2016 Olympic Games after finishing in the top four of their respective Sevens World Series competitions.

They were three great achievements, and once again underlined the strength in depth in English rugby.

It is of course Rugby World Cup year and although I cannot guarantee we will win the tournament, I can promise England will be in the best possible shape to challenge for the Webb Ellis Trophy.

When I became head coach we, firstly, had to win back public confidence in the team. Secondly, we had to build a strong culture within the squad. Thirdly, we had to forge attacking and defensive structures that could be effective against the very best sides in the world.

I can confidently say we have done all of those things.

The players, coaches and management team carry the expectations of the country on our shoulders. It is a privilege and an honour.

We all remember where we were when Jonny Wilkinson kicked that drop-goal in 2003 and the effect it had on the country. We all know what it would mean if we could do something similar this time.

Of course, this tournament stretches beyond the England team. The best players and the best teams in the world will be on our shores, and from Exeter to Newcastle the rugby will be tremendous.

But when it comes to our prospects of achieving our goal and winning the tournament at Twickenham on October 31, we need your support. We require your help, be it in the stadium, in your local club, or at home.

Best wishes,
Stuart Lancaster

Right: Stuart Lancaster is looking forward to his first Rugby World Cup campaign as England head coach.

Introduction

A year in which the England men's side again came agonisingly close to claiming the RBS 6 Nations title as the countdown to the Rugby World Cup gathered pace, 2015 also saw significant success for England's men in Sevens rugby and for the Under 20 side.

Despite leading both the try and points scoring tables in the tournament, Stuart Lancaster's side ultimately finished second in the RBS 6 Nations Championship, but had they been able to register just six more points in their five matches – or three against Ireland – they would have been crowned champions, ahead of the Irish, for the first time since 2011.

England, instead, had to be content with a fourth consecutive runners-up place, but there was much to enthuse about in the team's displays, not least their second-half revival against Wales in Cardiff's Millennium Stadium to win 21-16 and then their rampant 55-35 demolition of France at Twickenham on the final weekend of the tournament, the first time in the 109-year history of the fixture that they had scored a half-century of points against Les Bleus.

On the Sevens circuit, England's men and women prepared to kick-off their respective 2014-15 World Rugby Sevens Series campaigns in the unusual situation of carrying the weight of expectation of more than one country on their shoulders.

With the top four sides in each tournament earning automatic qualification for the Rio de Janeiro 2016 Olympic Games, England was charged with representing England, Wales and Scotland in the bid to seal a place in Brazil for Team GB.

Both Simon Amor's men side and Simon Middleton's women left it until the final event of their Series to confirm qualification but ultimately got the job done and, with rugby returning to the Olympic Games for the first time in 92 years in 2016, English players will now be part of the carnival in Brazil's second city.

Jon Callard's Under 20 side went into the Six Nations as world champions and they provided further proof of the continuing wealth of youthful talent in the domestic game by reclaiming the title they had ceded to France in 2014.

The youngsters began their campaign with a narrow defeat to Wales in Colwyn Bay, but recovered strongly to beat Italy, Ireland and Scotland, thus setting up a winner-takes-all clash with France on the final weekend.

They emerged from the clash in Brighton as 24-11 winners, establishing England Under 20s as the undisputed kings of both European and world rugby.

Elsewhere, the England Counties side recorded an unbeaten season after victories over their Scottish and French counterparts, while England Students emerged victorious from their Anglo-Welsh clash in Caerphilly with a 29-26 win.

For the women's teams, it was more of a struggle, but the 2014 Women's Rugby World Cup winners were in full rebuilding mode and the performances gave plenty of reasons for optimism in the years to come.

Right **The England team gave supporters plenty to cheer at Twickenham during their three home RBS 6 Nations Championship matches in 2015.**

Despite narrowly missing out on the Grand Slam, England gave their supporters plenty to cheer during the 2015 RBS 6 Nations Championship.

ENGLAND'S MEN IN 2015

Buoyed by beating Australia at Twickenham in their last Test outing of 2014, England regrouped in 2015 in optimistic mood and determined to build on the progress made under Stuart Lancaster. Another year of significant challenges lay ahead especially with key members of the squad battling injuries. Nonetheless, with a powerful pack and a cutting edge out wide, the men in white looked well equipped to deal with everything thrown at them.

RBS 6 NATIONS 2015

England's last competitive action before the start of the Rugby World Cup, the 2015 RBS 6 Nations Championship campaign was a final opportunity for Stuart Lancaster and his coaching staff to fine tune preparations for the bid to lift the Webb Ellis Cup later in the year.

Since being crowned RBS 6 Nations champions in 2011, England had registered three successive second place finishes, but hopes were high the team could go one better in 2015.

They came agonisingly close, only to lose out, once again, to Ireland on points difference, but England's haul of 18 tries and 157 points in five Tests, including victory against Wales in Cardiff and a record-breaking win over France at Twickenham, were testament to the team's potential.

Captain Chris Robshaw lifted the Calcutta Cup after his side's 25–13 victory at Twickenham in March, England's sixth consecutive win against Scotland.

Wales vs England

GLORY IN CARDIFF

With painful memories of their 30-3 mauling in the Millennium Stadium in 2013 still fresh, England headed to the Principality in early February desperate to begin the Championship in style. England had registered just one victory in their last six visits to the Welsh capital but an irresistible second-half fightback under the floodlights in Cardiff ensured Stuart Lancaster's side emerged worthy winners.

England
Rugby

Wales 16
England 21

Date: **6 February 2015**
Stadium: **Millennium Stadium, Cardiff**
Attendance: **73,815**
Referee: **Jerome Garces (France)**

The importance of strength in depth in modern Test rugby cannot be overstated. The attritional nature of the professional game makes injuries inevitable and as England prepared for their eagerly-anticipated meeting with Wales, Lancaster surveyed a squad ravaged by withdrawals and players reluctantly confined to the treatment room.

The list of walking wounded was certainly extensive. Manu Tuilagi, Owen Farrell, David Wilson, Joe Launchbury, Courtney Lawes, Tom Wood and Ben Morgan were all unavailable and when Lancaster unveiled his starting XV for Cardiff, there were only nine survivors from the team which had defeated Australia at HQ in November.

The enforced changes meant five players – the Bath quartet of wing Anthony Watson, centre Jonathan Joseph, fly-half George Ford and second row Dave Attwood, as well as Saracens lock George Kruis – would be making their first RBS 6 Nations start while Leicester prop Dan Cole was recalled to the side for the first time since he had

Left: **Bath wing Anthony Watson scored England's first try in the Millennium Stadium in their RBS 6 Nations Championship opener against Wales.**

featured against Scotland 12 months earlier.

On the bench there was a return to arms for 36-year-old Harlequins No 8 Nick Easter for the first time since the 2011 World Cup campaign while three British & Irish Lions - hooker Tom Youngs, prop Mako Vunipola and flanker Tom Croft – were also named by Lancaster among the England replacements.

The prematch build-up however was dominated by reflection on the match in Cardiff two years earlier and debate whether England still carried any psychological scars from that chastening defeat. The England camp did not shy away from the inevitable questions but there was quiet sense of confidence as the match drew closer.

"That day hurt quite a lot," conceded Mike Catt, the attacking skills coach. "Every English person hurt that day - it wasn't just the team. But it was two years ago. Since then as a team we have been successful against Wales and we are excited. We are looking forward to it. It won't happen again because we are two years more experienced and the group of players have been in big cauldrons in New Zealand and South Africa. Those things will stand us in good stead."

Even with its roof firmly open on England's insistence, the Millennium

Stadium was a cauldron of noise on Friday evening as referee Jérôme Garcès signalled the start of the match and as they had done in the fixture in 2013, it was home side who drew first blood when full-back Leigh Halfpenny landed an early penalty.

The score was the catalyst for a sustained Welsh onslaught and England were firmly on the back foot after seven minutes when number eight Toby Faletau burst from the back of an attacking scrum and deftly created space for scrum-half Rhys Webb on the blindside to touch down for the opening try of the match.

England supporters could have been forgiven for fearing a repeat of 2013 but the team proved their mettle with an intelligently crafted try of their own in the 14th minute which abruptly arrested the Welsh momentum. England moved the ball wide in the opposition 22 and as the defence rushed up to close down the space, Mike Brown opted for a teasing grubber kicker behind the defensive line. Wales turned desperately but it was Watson who was quickest to the bouncing ball, outpacing the Welsh defenders to dab down in the corner for the first Test try of his career.

Ford missed the conversion but was on target with a penalty in the 31st minute.

Below left: Jonathan Joseph's first Test try helped secure a famous 21-16 victory for Stuart Lancaster's team in Cardiff.

Below right: Making only his third Test start, fly-half George Ford was in imperious form for England against Wales.

Wales fly-half Dan Biggar stretched the home side's advantage with a first-half injury time drop goal and as the two sides headed to their respective dressing rooms, England found themselves 16-8 adrift.

The match was now firmly in the balance but it was England who dramatically seized the initiative just three minutes after the restart with a superbly worked try. After 19 phases of patient play, the Red Rose found themselves just metres from the Wales line, the ball at Ben Youngs' feet after another successful ruck. The Tigers scrum-half looked right and span possession wide to Joseph and his combination of upper body strength and a dummy to the supporting Brown saw the Bath centre beat three Welsh defenders for the score. This time Ford was able to add the two extra points and after trailing by 10 points early in the first half, Lancaster's team were now just 16-15 in arrears.

They surged into the lead for the first time in the contest in the 61st minute when Ford landed a second penalty and by this stage it was the Red Rose who were in the ascendency in terms of possession and territory, keeping Wales caged in their own half for long periods.

The match however was not yet won. Ford's third penalty two minutes from time

Above: **England's dramatic second–half fightback in the Millennium Stadium earned them a first victory in the Welsh capital in four years.**

"This win is definitely one of the highest points because of the pressure and emotion leading up into it and getting new combinations together."

Stuart Lancaster

– a glorious effort from 45 metres – gave England a five-point cushion and a degree of breathing space but there was still time for the home side to score a converted try which would have snatched victory from the jaws of defeat.

After their second-half recovery, it would have been a cruel blow had the home side managed to conjure up the seven points they needed but the Red Rose defence held firm as the seconds ticked by and when Garcès' whistle sounded for the final time, Lancaster and his players were able to celebrate a superb 21-16 triumph.

It was a result – the first time England had ever beaten Wales in Cardiff after trailing at half time - which underlined the progress England had made under Lancaster and with the two sides scheduled to meet again in the pool stages of the World Cup at Twickenham later in the year, a significant step forward for the men in white.

The head coach acknowledged victory was arguably the highlight of his three-year tenure of the team but was reluctant to read too much into it in terms of the World Cup and the rematch in late September.

"I remember being interviewed after the game two years ago and that was the lowest point of my coaching career without a doubt," Lancaster said in Cardiff. "We learned a lot from two years ago and drew a lot of strength from last year's performance against Wales [at Twickenham] and the way we finished the autumn series against Australia. This win is definitely one of the highest points because of the pressure and emotion leading up into it and getting new combinations together.

"We made a few changes but we knew we had a good side and we knew if we stuck to the plan we would cause Wales problems. We were under pressure to chase the game but I don't think we did. We got into the right field position and the physicality of our power runners ultimately made the difference. The World Cup is a long way off and this was about getting the victory for that young team away from home. It's great for us in terms of belief."

Wales 16 — England 21

Wales 16		England 21	
15	Leigh HALFPENNY	15	Mike BROWN
14	Alex CUTHBERT	14	Anthony WATSON
13	Jonathan DAVIES	13	Jonathan JOSEPH
12	Jamie ROBERTS	12 →	Luther BURRELL
11 →	George NORTH	11	Jonny MAY
10	Dan BIGGAR	10	George FORD
9 →	Rhys WEBB	9 →	Ben YOUNGS
1 →	Gethin JENKINS	1 →	Joe MARLER
2	Richard HIBBARD	2 →	Dylan HARTLEY
3 →	Samson LEE	3 →	Dan COLE
4 →	Jake BALL	4	Dave ATTWOOD
5	Alun Wyn JONES	5 →	George KRUIS
6	Dan LYDIATE	6	James HASKELL
7	Sam WARBURTON (c)	7	Chris Robshaw (c)
8	Toby FALETAU	8	Billy VUNIPOLA

REPLACEMENTS

	Wales		England
	16 Scott BALDWIN	2 ←	16 Tom YOUNGS
1 ←	17 Paul JAMES	1 ←	17 Mako VUNIPOLA
3 ←	18 Aaron JARVIS	3 ←	18 Kieran BROOKES
4 ←	19 Luke CHARTERIS	5 ←	19 Nick EASTER
	20 Justin TIPURIC		20 Tom CROFT
9 ←	21 Mike PHILLIPS	9 ←	21 Richard WIGGLESWORTH
	22 Rhys PRIESTLAND		22 Danny CIPRIANI
11 ←	23 Liam WILLIAMS	12 ←	23 Billy TWELVETREES

SCORES
Try: Webb (7)
Con: Halfpenny (8)
Pens: Halfpenny (1, 23)
Drop: Biggar (40)

SCORES
Tries: Watson (14), Joseph (43)
Con: Ford (45)
Pens: Ford (31, 61, 78)

Wales		England
32	Kicks from hand	32
121	Passes	118
109	Carries	132
224	Metres made	350
51%	Possession	49%
45%	Territory	55%
2	Clean breaks	3
14	Defenders beaten	21
6	Offloads	9
83 from 88	Rucks won	87 from 91
4	Mauls won	9
11	Turnovers conceded	14
135 (21)	Tackles (missed)	145 (14)
87%	Tackling success rate	91%
6/2 (75%)	Scrums won/lost	3/0 (100%)
10/4 (72%)	Lineouts won/lost	9/2 (82%)
9 (1)	Penalties conceded (freekicks)	9 (0)
1/0	Yellow/red cards	0/0

England vs Italy

JOSEPH DOUBLE SINKS ITALY

Buoyed by their superb fightback in Cardiff, Stuart Lancaster's squad steeled themselves for the second weekend of the championship and the challenge of Jacques Brunel's Italy, looking for their first victory over England in 21 Tests.

England
Rugby

England 47

Italy 17

Date: **14 February 2015**
Stadium: **Twickenham,**
London
Attendance: **82,061**
Referee: **John Lacey**
(Ireland)

All coaches crave continuity. The luxury of being able to select an unchanged XV for successive Tests is rare but with no fresh injuries to contend with after the Wales game, it was just this elusive scenario that presented itself to Lancaster as he considered his options for the Italy game and the second chapter of the 2105 RBS 6 Nations Championship.

It came as no surprise then that the head coach decided to keep faith with the same starting line-up. His heroes from the Millennium Stadium were selected en bloc and with the news that Lions and Leicester lock Geoff Parling had failed to recover from a knee injury, it was also the same

eight replacements from Cardiff on the bench, too.

England's historical domination of Italy over the years, and the display at the Millennium Stadium, convinced many that victory would be a mere formality, but assistant coach Andy Farrell was quick to dispel such presumptuous talk.

"We know the game always takes its own way," he said. "What we have to do is be good enough to feel the momentum of the game and how to influence it. The performance will come on the back of that really.

"To have a fixed plan of how it will unfold in your head before the game isn't reality. If Italy turn up and play exceptionally well, it

will be a really tough game, there's no doubt about that.

"In the 6 Nations you have to make sure that mentally and emotionally you're in the right place to put your plan into action on the field. That's important against Italy as well because let's not forget that it was a cup final for everyone last weekend. To win a Championship you have five of those cup finals.

"Earlier in the week we showed the players what they did well against Wales and what they didn't do well. Mentally we brought them down a bit and then built them back up again. Hopefully against Italy we'll be at that cup final stage again. There's a feel good factor around the rugby country at this moment but we need to back up the Wales performance."

The feel good factor however was initially in danger of evaporating at Twickenham as Italy came out fighting and captain Sergio Parisse powered his way over for a try after only five minutes.

But with the crowd behind them, England rallied with a George Ford penalty midway through the first half, but it was not until the 23rd minute that the HQ faithful were able to breathe a little more easily.

Lineout ball was secured five metres from the Italian line and Billy Vunipola went charging down the blindside. A combination of Parisse and scrum-half Edoardo Gori seemed to have manhandled the Saracens number eight into touch, but referee John Lacey consulted with the Television Match Official. When the replays were shown, they showed Vunipola had managed to touch down the ball before going over the touchline.

The opening try steadied English nerves and, three minutes later, they created another score. Skipper Chris Robshaw ripped possession from Italy at the breakdown, Ben Youngs spun the ball wide to Dan Cole and after touches from George Ford and Luther Burrell, Jonathan Joseph found himself on the halfway line.

With a mesmeric step inside then out, the Bath centre carved open a space between three Italian defenders and accelerated. The cover in the shape of *Azzurri* wing Leonardo Sarto came across but Joseph

Left: **Nick Easter, on the ground between Tom Youngs (16) and Billy Vunipola (8), is awarded England's sixth and final try against Italy.**

Right: **Danny Cipriani scored one of England's six tries at Twickenham in his first RBS 6 Nations Championship appearance for the men in white since 2008.**

was too fleet-footed and he went over beneath the posts for a dazzling solo score.

It was 15-5 to the home side at the break but Italy valiantly hit back early in the second half with a Luca Morisi score to reduce the deficit. The subsequent 14 minutes however belonged to England as Lancaster's side cut loose with four tries to spectacularly settle the contest.

The first went to Youngs in the 54th minute. England's impressive front row earned the side a penalty at a scrum three metres from the Italian line and as the visitors retreated lethargically, the Leicester nine tapped and dived through the tackle of Mauro Bergamasco for the try.

Six minutes later England went over again, and it came courtesy of another sublime display of raw pace and poise from Joseph. From the base of an England scrum on halfway, replacement Billy Twelvetrees quickly moved the ball wide to Ford, who delayed a deft pass to Joseph by a split-second. The deception froze the Italian midfield, opening up a gap, Joseph scorched his way through it for his second long range try of the match.

Holding a 35-10 lead, Lancaster turned to the replacements bench and it was one of the substitutes – Danny Cipriani – who made the next significant contribution with only

his second touch of the ball. After England had stolen lineout possession on the 10-metre line, Cipriani fed Twelvetrees who, in turn, found Jonny May on the left wing. The *Azzurri* defence seemed well organised, but May's electrifying burst of acceleration committed three tacklers to him. As May was hauled down, he saw Cipriani on his inside shoulder and the pass gave him a clear route to the line.

The irresistible scoring salvo came to an end in the 68th minute. Tom Croft rose highest at a lineout eight metres short of the line to secure possession and the pack advanced with a rolling maul. It came to a halt in a mass of bodies over the Italian try line and as the two sets of forwards disentangled themselves, it was Harlequins No 8 Nick Easter with the smile on his face.

There was time for one final score but it went to the visitors, two minutes from the end, when Morisi crashed over for his second try. It was no more than a consolation and when Lacey signalled full time, England were 47-17 winners.

There was no argument about the recipient of the Man-of-the-Match accolade at Twickenham. Joseph's two tries were both sensational efforts and for many England supporters of a certain vintage, his

performance was reminiscent of another legendary Bath centre, Jeremy Guscott.

"It's great to be compared to someone like him," Joseph said. "He was a player with such class and ability who had such a great career with Bath and England.

"It's up to me to keep working hard and keep my feet on the ground. I am not the finished article and can get better. I just want to try to be the best I can. It felt great to get two tries in an England win but things move on quickly and you can't sit back and relax.

"I've found that if I stay close to George [Ford], he usually creates something for me. Credit to him today because he helped me go over the whitewash.

"Missing out on [on the tour of] New Zealand last year was a big blow for me. But missing that opportunity made me even more determined to get where I wanted to be."

> "I am not the finished article and I can get better. It felt great to get two tries in an England win but you can't sit back and relax"
>
> **Jonathan Joseph**

England 47 — Italy 17

#	England 47	#	Italy 17
15	Mike BROWN	15	Luke McLEAN
14	Anthony WATSON	14	Leonardo SARTO
13	Jonathan JOSEPH	13	Luca MORISI
12	Luther BURRELL	12	Andrea MASI
11	Jonny MAY	11	Giovanbattista VENDITTI
10	George FORD	10	Kelly HAIMONA
9	Ben YOUNGS	9	Edoardo GORI
1	Joe MARLER	1	Alberto DE MARCHI
2	Dylan HARTLEY	2	Leonardo GHIRALDINI
3	Dan COLE	3	Martin CASTROGIOVANNI
4	Dave ATTWOOD	4	George BIAGI
5	George KRUIS	5	Marco BORTOLAMI
6	James HASKELL	6	Francesco MINTO
7	Chris ROBSHAW (C)	7	Mauro BERGAMASCO
8	Billy VUNIPOLA	8	Sergio PARISSE (C)

REPLACEMENTS

	England		Italy
2	16 Tom YOUNGS	2	16 Andrea MANICI
1	17 Mako VUNIPOLA	1	17 Matias AGUERO
3	18 Kieran BROOKES	3	18 Dario CHISTOLINI
4	19 Nick EASTER	5	19 Josh FURNO
5	20 Tom CROFT	7	20 Samuela VUNISA
9	21 Richard WIGGLESWORTH	9	21 Guglielmo PALAZZANI
10	22 Danny CIPRIANI	10	22 Tommaso ALLAN
15	23 Billy TWELVETREES	14	23 Giulio BISEGNI

SCORES

Tries: B Vunipola (23), Joseph (26, 60), B Youngs (54), Cipriani (63), Easter (68)
Cons: Ford (28, 55, 62), Cipriani (63)
Pens: Ford (20, 45, 57)

Tries: Parisse (3), Morisi (49, 78)
Con: Allan (79)

England	Statistic	Italy
27	Kicks from hand	16
155	Passes	154
106	Runs	127
530	Metres run with ball	285
47%	Possession	53%
47%	Territory	53%
9	Clean breaks	11
19	Defenders beaten	26
10	Offloads	9
71 from 73	Rucks won	94 from 99
4	Mauls won	0
9	Turnovers conceded	18
164 (26)	Tackles (made/missed)	113 (19)
86%	Tackling success rate	86%
6/1 (86%)	Scrums on own feed	4/1 (80%)
11/1 (92%)	Lineouts on own throw	7/3 (70%)
7 (0)	Penalties conceded (freekicks)	10 (0)
0/0	Yellow/red cards	0/0

Ireland vs England

AVIVA ANGUISH

A clash featuring the last two unbeaten sides in the championship, England travelled to Dublin to face the defending RBS 6 Nations champions. Although there had been four successive victories over Ireland, the one over Joe Schmidt's team at Twickenham in 2014 had been very narrow (13-10), so England were under no illusions that this was their sternest examination in the tournament so far.

England Rugby

Ireland 19
England 9

Date: **1 March 2015**
Stadium: **Aviva Stadium, Dublin**
Attendance: **51,200**
Referee: **Craig Joubert (South Africa)**

Talk of potential Grand Slams were banished from the respective camps in the build-up to the clash in the Aviva Stadium, but both Stuart Lancaster and Schmidt – in private at least – knew victory in Dublin would represent a significant step towards a coveted Championship clean sweep.

The scale of the challenge faced by England to take that step was considerable. Ireland boasted a formidable nine Test winning streak before kick-off and fresh from their victory over the French in Paris, they were not short of confidence.

The same, of course, was true of England after the impressive defeat of Italy at Twickenham a fortnight earlier. The victory extended their RBS 6 Nations Championship winning sequence to six matches, so this meeting with Ireland pitted two in-form sides.

Lancaster made two changes to his starting line-up to face Ireland from the one that had beaten both Wales and Italy, one of which was enforced. Mike Brown had sustained a concussion early in the match against Italy, but a setback in his rehabilitation forced him to miss out, so Saracens full-back Alex Goode was chosen for his 16th cap, but his first start since March 2013.

Left: **England's match in Dublin was the fourth time skipper Chris Robshaw (running with the ball) had faced Ireland in a Test match.**

Right: **England's lineout came under severe pressure from Ireland in the Aviva Stadium, but Dave Attwood gathered this one safely.**

"Our biggest disappointment was our discipline. You don't want to give them easy opportunities and allow them to keep the scoreboard ticking over."

Chris Robshaw

The other change was tactical and, after careful consideration, Lancaster decided Exeter's Jack Nowell, an ever-present during the 2014 RBS 6 Nations, was worthy of a recall and he replaced Jonny May on the left wing.

There was one alteration on the replacements bench with Bath prop Henry Thomas, having recovered from a hip injury, taking over from Kieran Brookes.

"We've made minimal changes as we felt the squad performed well in the first two games," Lancaster explained. "Alex is in good form for Saracens and has been training well over the last few weeks. He's played for us in big internationals and while he's a slightly different type of player, he certainly brings a lot to the party.

"Jack's consistency for his club has been very good. He rarely makes an error. He's very good under the high ball and is good defensively."

The atmosphere inside the Aviva Stadium before kick-off was electric, reflecting the importance of the match, and buoyed by their vociferous home support Ireland started the stronger of the two teams, taking an early 6-0 lead with two penalties inside the opening eight minutes from fly-half Jonathan Sexton.

England responded three minutes later with a series of powerful drives in the Irish 22. Referee Craig Joubert signalled for a penalty advantage for not rolling away but, rather than calling for the kicking tee, fly-half George Ford took Ben Youngs' pinpoint pass and knocked over a drop goal to open England's account.

A third Sexton penalty on the half hour mark restored the home side's six-point advantage and when the half-time whistle sounded, Ireland were 9-3 in front.

Significantly the first score of the second period went to Ireland, seven minutes after the restart. England's forwards were caught offside and Sexton was on target with his fourth successful penalty.

However, the defining moment of the match came in the 52nd minute, when the home side registered the game's only try. England, under severe pressure inside their own 22. This time Joubert signalled a penalty advantage to the Irish. Although the defence was holding firm, Irish scrum-half Conor Murray sent a speculative box kick to the corner, safe in the knowledge that Sexton would still have the chance to kick the penalty to make it 15-3.

Goode was seemingly perfectly positioned in the dead ball area to deal with the threat, but Ireland centre Robbie Henshaw came from the England full-back's blind side, challenged for the ball in the air, beat him to it and touched down as he hit the ground. The Television Match Official confirmed Henshaw had grounded the ball successfully before Sexton added the touchline conversion to make it 19-3.

The fightback that ensued was both courageous and thrilling, but ultimately not enough to avoid defeat. A Ford penalty

in the 58th minute helped to steady the England ship and the team began to generate real momentum in the final quarter. Another penalty was kicked by the nerveless Bath youngster after muscular contributions from Dan Cole and then Billy Vunipola around the fringes.

The deficit was down to 10 points and, in the closing stages, England threw everything at Ireland in a desperate bid to overhaul the champions. A probing burst from Nowell in the opposition 22 put England on the front foot. Skipper Chris Robshaw provided continuity with a pick and go from the resulting breakdown and it took three desperate tackles to stop substitute Tom Croft, winning his 40th cap from the bench, just a metre short of the line.

England came again even as the clock ticked down and, in the final minute, appeared to have scored the try their collective efforts deserved. The forwards were halted five metres from the line, replacement scrum-half Richard Wigglesworth fizzed the ball left and it quickly moved to Billy Twelvetrees, making a curving run outside the congested Irish midfield.

Twelvetrees passed to Nowell, who dived low into the corner before the covering tacklers could bundle him into touch. Joy

Left: **Ireland centre Robbie Henshaw scored the only try of the match as Joe Schmidt's team ran out 19–9 winners in Dublin.**

Right: **Exeter wing Jack Nowell faced a testing 80 minutes under the high ball against the reigning RBS 6 Nations champions in the Aviva Stadium.**

quickly turned to dismay, however, when Joubert ruled the pass from Twelvetrees was forward. He then blew for full time, giving England no time to mount another attack.

Ireland's four-match losing sequence against England was over, Lancaster and his team had to reflect on a defeat defined by frustratingly small margins, including an uncharacteristically high penalty count and Sexton's unerringly accurate kicking display.

"Our biggest disappointment was our discipline," Robshaw admitted. "When Ireland have a serious player like Jonathan Sexton, who can nail goals and pin you in the corner, you don't want to give them any easy opportunities and allow them to keep the scoreboard ticking over.

"We conceded some penalties due to pressure and some due to our own loss in concentration. As a team you aim for under 10 penalties; that's the benchmark for the 80 minutes. If you do that, you're in a good place. We gave away eight penalties in the first half and that pressure tells.

"We now have to put all of our attention into Scotland, and see what happens in the last two games. Credit to Ireland – they played well and were pretty smart about how they went about their business. They got the better of us. We were slightly off and they exploited us."

Ireland 19	England 9
15 Rob **KEARNEY**	15 Alex **GOODE**
14 Tommy **BOWE**	14 Anthony **WATSON**
13 → Jared **PAYNE**	13 → Jonathan **JOSEPH**
12 Robbie **HENSHAW**	12 Luther **BURRELL**
11 Simon **ZEBO**	11 Jack **NOWELL**
10 → Jonathan **SEXTON**	10 George **FORD**
9 Conor **MURRAY**	9 → Ben **YOUNGS**
1 → Jack **McGRATH**	1 → Joe **MARLER**
2 Rory **BEST**	2 → Dylan **HARTLEY**
3 Mike **ROSS**	3 Dan **COLE**
4 → Devin **TONER**	4 → Dave **ATTWOOD**
5 Paul **O'CONNELL** (C)	5 George **KRUIS**
6 Peter **O'MAHONY**	6 → James **HASKELL**
7 → Sean **O'BRIEN**	7 Chris **ROBSHAW** (C)
8 Jordi **MURPHY**	8 Billy **VUNIPOLA**

REPLACEMENTS	REPLACEMENTS
2 ← 16 Sean **CRONIN**	2 ← 16 Tom **YOUNGS**
1 ← 17 Cian **HEALY**	1 ← 17 Mako **VUNIPOLA**
3 ← 18 Marty **MOORE**	18 Henry **THOMAS**
4 ← 19 Iain **HENDERSON**	4 ← 19 Nick **EASTER**
7 ← 20 Tommy **O'DONNELL**	6 ← 20 Tom **CROFT**
21 Eoin **REDDAN**	9 ← 21 Richard **WIGGLESWORTH**
10 ← 22 Ian **MADIGAN**	22 Danny **CIPRIANI**
13 ← 23 Felix **JONES**	13 ← 23 Billy **TWELVETREES**

SCORES

SCORES

Try: **Henshaw** (52)

Con: **Sexton** (53)

Pens: **Sexton** (1, 8, 29, 47)

Pens: **Ford** (58, 67)

Drop: **Ford** (11)

Ireland		England
38	Kicks from hand	23
156	Passes	120
135	Runs	124
300	Metres run with ball	501
59%	Possession	41%
59%	Territory	41%
3	Clean breaks	10
23	Defenders beaten	27
5	Offloads	8
116/118	Rucks won	85/92
4	Mauls won	3
9	Turnovers conceded	23
120 (27)	Tackles (made/missed)	160 (23)
82%	Tackling success rate	87%
6/2 (75%)	Scrums on own feed	2/0 (100%)
11/1 (92%)	Lineouts on own throw	10/3 (77%)
8 (2)	Penalties conceded (freekicks)	13 (2)
0/0	Yellow/red cards	0/0

England v Scotland

CALCUTTA CUP TRIUMPH

The 133rd instalment of the oldest fixture in Test Rugby, the 2015 clash for the Calcutta Cup brought together two teams who had experienced disappointing defeats a fortnight earlier. For England, it was an opportunity to reignite their title ambitions; for Scotland, it represented a chance to register a first victory in the championship.

England
Rugby

England 25
Scotland 13

Date: **14 March 2015**
Stadium: **Twickenham,**
   London
Attendance: **82,284**
Referee: **Romain Poite**
   (France)

As the two sides prepared to renew their annual Anglo-Scottish rivalry, the omens for an England win at Twickenham were certainly encouraging. Their last defeat to Scotland at HQ had come back in 1983 and with Vern Cotter's side reeling from successive RBS 6 Nations defeats to France, Wales and Italy, Stuart Lancaster's team were installed as short favourites to extend their 16-match unbeaten sequence against Scotland on home soil.

The sense of optimism ahead of the match was bolstered by the return of a quartet of senior players, Tom Wood, Courtney Lawes, Geoff Parling and Mike Brown, to full fitness but Lancaster resisted the temptation to parachute all of them back into his starting XV en masse.

Fully recovered from the concussion he suffered in the Italy game, Brown was recalled at full-back in place of Alex Goode. Lawes was also reinstated in the second row after recovering from an ankle problem to win his 37th cap at the expense of George Kruis, but Wood and Parling had to settle for a place on the England bench, Nick Easter and Tom Croft dropping out of the matchday 23.

Another change saw Newcastle prop Kieran Brookes replace Henry Thomas among the replacements but, as kick-off approached, it was an England

Left: **George Ford's second-half try against Scotland at Twickenham was the first of the young fly-half's international career**

Above: **Jonathan Joseph's early score at Twickenham took his try haul in the 2015 RBS 6 Nations Championship to four in four appearances.**

squad determined to put their Dublin disappointment firmly behind them.

"Coming off the back of a loss, we know that we need a big performance and a big result," said fly-half George Ford before the game. "We've trained that way, and are all very much looking forward to it. We're going into the game looking for a really good performance but foremost we need the win. Whatever way we get that, it's vital we get it.

"We did a lot of good things against Ireland in the last 20 minutes but it's about doing it for the full 80 minutes [against Scotland] and going out there and enjoying ourselves. We lost in Dublin and we didn't play to our best, but still we have a very positive mindset going into the last two games. We did a lot of good things in the opening three games and still have a chance of winning the Championship."

By any measure, England started the match at a blistering pace at Twickenham and it took them just four minutes to breach the Scottish defence for the first time.

The move began with quick ruck ball on the Scotland 22. Ben Youngs found Billy Vunipola on a trademark charge and after

> "It was really important for us to bounce back from the Ireland defeat. We got the result we wanted and we move on to France next week."
>
> **Ben Youngs**

he was hauled down, the pack powered on, with James Haskell making more hard metres. Youngs' pinpoint pass from the base went to Ford, and he, in turn, fed Jonathan Joseph, who sliced through the visitors' midfield on the angle, deftly sidestepping full-back Stuart Hogg for his fourth try in four appearances in the tournament. Ford was on target with the conversion and with some of the 82,284-strong crowd still finding their seats, England were already 7-0 in front.

England were rampant and only a last ditch tackle by Hogg on Brown in the 12th minute, two metres short of the line, denied England a second try.

Scotland however forced their way back into the contest midway through the half with their first attack of the game, a drive from lock Richie Gray putting England on the back foot before centre Mark Bennett was able to muscle his way over for a converted try in the right-hand corner.

England thought they had recaptured the lead when Anthony Watson galloped over the line on the half-hour mark, but referee Romain Poite brought them back for a forward pass in the build-up, After two penalties from Scotland captain Greig Laidlaw to one from Ford, the England headed in at half-time trailing 13-10 despite all their attacking verve.

Exactly what was said in the England dressing room at the break remained private, but Lancaster's side emerged for the second half with the same intent they had shown at the start of the match and it took them only three minutes to unlock the Scottish defence once again.

The forwards did the preparatory work inside the opposition 22 and Youngs

orchestrated the attack left. Brown was stopped five metres short but was able to offload in the tackle and, this time, Youngs went right, finding captain Chris Robshaw in midfield. The captain caught and offloaded to Ford in one movement. It allowed the fly-half to dummy and ghost over beneath

Below: **Jack Nowell's try against Scotland was his second in the RBS 6 Nations Championship.**

Bottom: **England's Calcutta Cup win meant they could still win the RBS 6 Nations title**

the posts. The conversion sailed over and England were back in the lead.

Another forward pass on the hour mark – this time from James Haskell to Brown – denied England a third try, but it was only a temporary reprieve for the Scots, and it arrived five minutes from the final whistle.

A series of drives from the forwards – two from Brookes and one from Vunipola – weakened Scottish resolve. When the ball was made available, Brown passed to Ford, and he delivered a long, flat pass to Jack Nowell, who had been a constant threat throughout the match. Despite the attentions of two Scotland players, the Exeter wing was able to touch down in the left corner for the second try of his England career.

The attempted touchline conversion from Ford was off-target, but England had done enough to retain the Calcutta Cup with a 25-13 victory and give themselves a chance of winning the Championship going into the following weekend's final round of matches and their clash with the French.

By the team's own admission, it had been a performance full of admirable attacking play – they made 17 clean line breaks and ran the ball for more than 600 metres – but the players conceded they should have converted more of their forays into scores.

"It was really important to us to bounce back from the Ireland defeat and I think we did that, but there was also some disappointing elements in our game," said Ben Youngs, who was named Man of the Match. "We missed a lot of opportunities and left a lot of points out there.

"There's relief in the end because we didn't want them to come back and bite us, missing those chances. However there's plenty to look at and we need to capitalise on those mistakes and those opportunities we're creating but not taking.

"We're happy with the result but in terms of performance there's a lot more to come. Scotland are a very good team and we've got a lot of respect for them. They came back at us but if we'd taken those opportunities and been a little more clinical it could have been a different game. We got the result we wanted and we move on to France next week."

England 25 — Scotland 13

England 25	Scotland 13
15 → Mike BROWN	15 Stuart HOGG
14 Anthony WATSON	14 Dougie FIFE
13 Jonathan JOSEPH	13 Mark BENNETT
12 Luther BURRELL	12 → Matt SCOTT
11 Jack NOWELL	11 Tommy SEYMOUR
10 → George FORD	10 → Finn RUSSELL
9 → Ben YOUNGS	9 Greig LAIDLAW (c)
1 → Joe MARLER	1 → Alasdair DICKINSON
2 → Dylan HARTLEY	2 → Ross FORD
3 → Dan COLE	3 → Euan MURRAY
4 → Dave ATTWOOD	4 → Jim HAMILTON
5 Courtney LAWES	5 Jonny GRAY
6 → James HASKELL	6 → Robert HARLEY
7 Chris ROBSHAW (c)	7 Blair COWAN
8 Billy VUNIPOLA	8 → David DENTON

REPLACEMENTS

REPLACEMENTS	REPLACEMENTS
2 ← 16 Tom YOUNGS	2 ← 16 Fraser BROWN
1 ← 17 Mako VUNIPOLA	1 ← 17 Ryan GRANT
3 ← 18 Kieran BROOKES	3 ← 18 Geoff CROSS
4 ← 19 Geoff PARLING	4 ← 19 Tim SWINSON
6 ← 20 Tom WOOD	6 ← 20 Johnnie BEATTIE
9 ← 21 Richard WIGGLESWORTH	8 ← 21 Adam ASHE
10 ← 22 Danny CIPRIANI	10 ← 22 Sam HIDALGO-CLYNE
15 ← 23 Billy TWELVETREES	12 ← 23 Greig TONKS

SCORES

SCORES	SCORES
Tries: **Joseph (4), Ford (43), Nowell (75)**	Try: **Bennett (21)**
Cons: **Ford (5, 43)**	Con: **Laidlaw (22)**
Pens: **Ford (25, 50)**	Pens: **Laidlaw (29, 38)**

England		Scotland
24	Kicks from hand	30
163	Passes	133
128	Runs	122
611	Metres run with ball	372
46%	Possession	54%
52%	Territory	48%
17	Clean breaks	5
27	Defenders beaten	16
22	Offloads	13
73/5	Rucks won	86/2
6	Mauls won	7
17	Turnovers conceded	19
121 (16)	Tackles (made/missed)	125 (27)
88%	Tackling success rate	82%
3/1 (75%)	Scrums on own feed	7/2 (78%)
14/1 (93%)	Lineouts on own throw	10/0 (100%)
10 (0)	Penalties conceded (freekicks)	8 (1)
0/0	Yellow/red cards	0/0

England v France

TRIUMPH AND TEARS AT TWICKENHAM

The final match of the final day of the 2015 RBS 6 Nations Championship, saw England take to the field at Twickenham against France knowing victory by 26 points or more would secure the title for the first time in four years and propel Stuart Lancaster's side into the Rugby World Cup as champions of the northern hemisphere.

England Rugby

England 55
France 35

Date: **21 March 2015**
Stadium: **Twickenham,**
London
Attendance: **82,319**
Referee: **Nigel Owens**
(Wales)

It was to prove a long and incredible day of international rugby. All six teams were in action and four were still in contention to lift the trophy, so it always promised to be a dramatic climax to the tournament. What unfolded on 21 March 2015, dubbed "Super Saturday", exceeded even those lofty expectations.

The day began with Wales' hugely entertaining 61-20 victory over Italy in Rome, a result which thrust Warren Gatland's side into pole position at the top of the table. Two hours later, however, they were deposed as leaders by Ireland when the defending champions beat Scotland at Murrayfield, their 40-10 success in Edinburgh. It took Joe Schmidt's side above Wales, their points difference being 10 better.

Attention now turned to Twickenham. A victory for England against *Les Bleus* would leave them level with Wales and Ireland on eight points. A winning margin of 26 points would see Lancaster's team match Ireland's points-difference of +63, but as England had already scored more tries than the Irish, they would be crowned champions.

Left: **England supporters descended on Twickenham hoping to see their side beat France and claim the RBS 6 Nations title.**

Right: **Scrum-half Ben Youngs sparked an England try-feast when he pierced the French defence at HQ inside the first minute of play.**

The scene was set and it was a familiar looking XV that ran out at Twickenham. The only change from the previous weekend saw Leicester second row Geoff Parling replace Dave Atwood. Nick Easter was recalled to the bench, while Leicester prop Dan Cole was earning his 50th cap.

"Finishing off the tournament at home is going to be a great occasion," said Lancaster in the build-up. "The support against Scotland last week was fantastic and this weekend we really need the crowd to get behind the team and drive them forward in what will be an exciting finale to this year's Championship.

"Geoff did well off the bench against Scotland and, now that he has got some games under his belt, we feel it is the right time to start him and use his experience and quality in the starting line-up. The same goes for Nick Easter, who is a quality ball carrier and great defender, things we feel we'll need in the latter stages of the game."

> "I'm hugely proud of what that England team has shown today and throughout the championship. I've never seen a more courageous performance from a group of players."
>
> **Stuart Lancaster**

"It's a great achievement for Dan, especially coming back from his injury last year. He is one of the cornerstones of our squad and we all wish him all the best."

What followed at HQ was as spectacular as it was ultimately heartbreaking, but England's heroics will long in the memory of all those who witnessed proceedings.

England could not have made a better start. After only two minutes, Jonathan Joseph pounced on a wayward French pass on half-way and initiated the counter attack. Mike Brown and George Ford were both heavily involved and as France desperately scrambled back, it was scrum-half Ben Youngs who was on hand to pirouette over for the opening try.

Twickenham erupted, but hope turned to anxiety as the visitors hit back with scores from scrum-half Sebastian Tillous-Borde and wing Noa Nakaitaci to change the complexion of the match. England regrouped and a searing break from Youngs around the fringes paved the way for Anthony Watson to score in the right-hand corner. Youngs was then the beneficiary of a quick tap penalty taken by Brown, powering through a tackle beneath the uprights for his second try of the contest.

This powerful riposte saw Lancaster's team head to the dressing room at half-time with a 27-15 lead, an advantage they would

Left: **Billy Vunipola's second-half score from close range gave England renewed hope of winning the championship ahead of Ireland on points difference.**

Below: **England's victory at HQ was the first time they had scored more than 50 points against France but was not enough to claim the RBS 6 Nations title.**

not relinquish for the rest of the match. But the burning question, as the two teams emerged for the second 40 minutes, was whether England could score enough points to get a better difference than Ireland.

The half started badly. France moved into the 22 and a deft flick from hooker Guilhem Guirado sent centre Maxime Mermoz crashing over from short range but, once again, the home side came roaring back with two tries to reignite their title challenge.

The first came in the 46th minute, when Youngs once again lacerated the French defence and Ford appeared on his shoulder to take the scoring pass. The second try

followed six minutes later when sharp hands from Ford created space for wing Jack Nowell on the left.

The score was now 41-25 –10 points short of what was required – but disaster struck when James Haskell was shown a yellow card for a trip on French fly-half Jules Plisson. While he served his 10 minutes in the sin bin, the visitors scored two more tries through prop Vincent Debaty and replacement hooker Benjamin Kayser.

England, however, refused to buckle and, even with 14 men, repaired some of the damage when number eight Billy Vunipola muscled his way over from a couple of metres out. When England were restored to a full complement of players, the scoreboard read 48-35 to the home side.

The crowd screamed for more and their team obliged in the 74th minute with a seventh try. A solid England scrum in the French 22 saw Youngs go left to replacement Billy Twelvetrees, who then found Ford. As the fly-half assessed his options, Nowell came flying up on his left shoulder to take a delayed pass, sprint through the gap and score his second try. Ford converted so, with five minutes remaining, England's lead was 55-35 and they needed just one more converted try to win the Championship.

It was almost unbearable to watch as the clocked ticked down and as it inevitably turned red, England had France trapped just two metres from their own line but they could not steal possession and mount one last attack. *Les Bleus* kicked to touch, referee Nigel Owens signalled full time.

Although England had registered a half-century of points against the French for the first time, it was still not quite enough to deny Ireland the title, courtesy of their narrowly superior points difference. Lancaster's team were six points adrift of their target.

The dejected look on the faces of the England players at the end spoke volumes, but Lancaster was eager to focus on what had been a phenomenal, record-breaking performance at Twickenham rather than the disappointment of what was an agonising near miss in terms of silverware.

"I want to congratulate Ireland on the Championship," the head coach said. "I'm sure it was a tense affair for them watching up in Scotland. It was pretty tense here if I'm being honest. I said to the boys at the end of the game, I've never seen such a courageous performance from a group of players.

"I'm hugely proud of what that England team has shown today and throughout the Championship. We've come up short in the end but the mindset to play and the ability to go and keep going at a high-quality French team and score the tries that we did was a testament to the spirit and character that we've got. We were also backed up by 82,000 people in a sporting environment that I've never been in before. It was incredible."

England 55 | France 35

England 55	France 35
15 Mike BROWN	15 Scott SPEDDING
14 → Anthony WATSON	14 Yoann HUGET
13 Jonathan JOSEPH	13 Gael FICKOU
12 → Luther BURRELL	12 → Maxime MERMOZ
11 Jack NOWELL	11 Noa NAKAITACI
10 George FORD	10 → Jules PLISSON
9 → Ben YOUNGS	9 → Sebastien TILLOUS-BORDE
1 → Joe MARLER	1 → Vincent DEBATY
2 → Dylan HARTLEY	2 → Guilhem GUIRADO
3 → Dan COLE	3 → Nicolas MAS
4 → Geoff PARLING	4 Alexandre FLANQUART
5 Courtney LAWES	5 → Yoann MAESTRI
6 → James HASKELL (57)	6 Thierry DUSAUTOIR (c)
7 Chris ROBSHAW (c)	7 Bernard LEROUX
8 Billy VUNIPOLA	8 → Loann GOUJON

REPLACEMENTS	REPLACEMENTS
2 ← 16 Tom YOUNGS	2 ← 16 Benjamin KAYSER
1 ← 17 Mako VUNIPOLA	3 ← 17 Rabah SLIMANI
3 ← 18 Kieran BROOKES	1 ← 18 Uini ATONIO
4 ← 19 Nick EASTER	5 ← 19 Romain TAOFIFENUA
6 ← 20 Tom WOOD	8 ← 20 Damien CHOULY
9 ← 21 Richard WIGGLESWORTH	9 ← 21 Rory KOCKOTT
14 ← 22 Danny CIPRIANI	10 ← 22 Remi TALES
12 ← 23 Billy TWELVETREES	12 ← 23 Mathieu BASTAREAUD

SCORES

Tries: B Youngs (1, 35), Watson (30), Ford (46), Nowell (53, 74), B Vunipola (63)

Cons: Ford (3, 30, 36, 46, 54, 63, 75)

Pens: Ford (26, 40)

SCORES

Tries: Tillous-Borde (13), Nakaitaci (17), Mermoz (42), Debaty (59), Kayser (65))

Cons: Plisson (18, 42)

Pens: Plisson (10), Kockott (51)

England		France
30	Kicks from hand	26
143	Passes	169
115	Runs	147
651	Metres run with ball	708
43%	Possession	57%
47%	Territory	53%
15	Clean breaks	14
24	Defenders beaten	25
9	Offloads	17
74/3	Rucks won	101/8
4	Mauls won	3
16	Turnovers conceded	12
161 (25)	Tackles (made/missed)	104 (24)
87%	Tackling success rate	81%
3/0 (100%)	Scrums on own feed	5/2 (71%)
10/1 (91%)	Lineouts on own throw	18/1 (89%)
9 (0)	Penalties conceded (freekicks)	11 (1)
1/0	Yellow/red cards	0/0

2015 RBS 6 Nations Statistics

Final Table

TEAM	P	W	D	L	F	A	PD	TRIES	PTS
Ireland	5	4	0	1	119	56	63	8	8
England	5	4	0	1	157	100	57	18	8
Wales	5	4	0	1	146	93	53	13	8
France	5	2	0	3	103	101	2	9	4
Italy	5	1	0	4	62	182	-120	8	2
Scotland	5	0	0	5	73	128	-55	6	0

England Points Scorers

George **FORD**	75	(2T, 13C, 12P, 1DG)
Jonathan **JOSEPH**	20	(4T)
Ben **YOUNGS**	15	(3T)
Jack **NOWELL**	15	(3T)
Anthony **WATSON**	10	(2T)
Billy **VUNIPOLA**	10	(2T)
Danny **CIPRIANI**	7	(1T, 1C)
Nick **EASTER**	5	(1T)

> "That performance today [against France] was outstanding. You can't get away from that. The belief and the lessons learned that we'll get from that game will be second to none."
>
> **Andy Farrell**

Championship Appearances

5
Luther **BURRELL**
Dan **COLE**
George **FORD**
Dylan **HARTLEY**
James **HASKELL**
Jonathan **JOSEPH**
Joe **MARLER**
Chris **ROBSHAW**
Billy **VUNIPOLA**
Mako **VUNIPOLA**
Anthony **WATSON**
Richard **WIGGLESWORTH**
Ben **YOUNGS**
Tom **YOUNGS**

4
Dave **ATTWOOD**
Kieran **BROOKES**
Mike **BROWN**
Nick **EASTER**
Billy **TWELVETREES**

3
Danny **CIPRAINI**
George **KRUIS**
Jack **NOWELL**

2
Tom **CROFT**
Courtney **LAWES**
Jonny **MAY**
Geoff **PARLING**
Tom **WOOD**

1
Alex **GOODE**

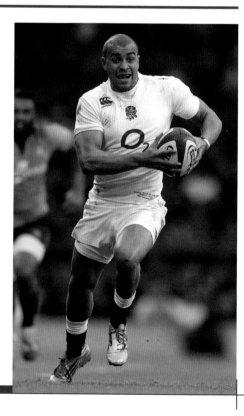

Right: Jonathan Joseph was the 2015 RBS 6 Nations Championship's leading try-scorer with four.

Team Tournament Records

Total Passes	699
Carries	605
Metres Made	2643
Offloads	58
Lineouts Won	54
Lineouts Lost	8
Rucks Won	390
Rucks Lost	21
Scrums Won	17
Scrums Lost	2
Turnovers Conceded	79
Defenders Beaten	118
Clean Breaks	54
Tackles Made	751
Tackles Missed	104
Yellow Cards	1
Red Cards	0

Individual Tournament Records

Most Metres	Jack **NOWELL**	326
Clean Breaks	Jack **NOWELL**	9
Top Try Scorer	Jonathan **JOSEPH**	4
Most Assists	George **FORD**	7
Kicks From Hand	George **FORD**	53
Defenders Beaten	Jack **NOWELL**	16
Most Carries	Billy **VUNIPOLA**	64
Most Tackles	Chris **ROBSHAW**	82
Lineout Steals	Dave **ATTWOOD**	3
Most Passes	Ben **YOUNGS**	280
Penalties Won	Luther **BURRELL**	2
	Tom **YOUNGS**	2
	Nick **EASTER**	2
	Dylan **HARTLEY**	2
	James **HASKELL**	2

Above: **Captain Chris Robshaw led by example during the championship with more successful tackles (82) than any other England player.**

IN PROFILE:

Jonathan Joseph

After almost two years without a cap, Jonathan Joseph exploded back onto the Test stage during the RBS 6 Nations with a series of mesmerising performances in England's midfield.

England Rugby

Position: **Centre**
Age: **24**
Height: **1.83m**
Weight: **91kg**
Caps: **11**
Points: **20 (4T)**

Second chances are rare in international rugby. The battle for Test places is relentlessly intense, and few players get the opportunity to resurrect their international careers. When the Bath centre was handed his chance by Stuart Lancaster in 2015, he grasped it spectacularly.

Before the start of this year's RBS 6 Nations, the 23-year-old had won seven caps, his debut being as a replacement against South Africa in Durban in June 2012. Joseph's seventh Test was a year later, against Argentina in Buenos Aries, but he could not cement his place in the team and had yet to register a Test match try.

That changed in January, when Lancaster selected him for the opening RBS 6 Nations fixture against Wales in Cardiff. He earned the recall after a series of dazzling performances for Bath Rugby in the Aviva Premiership and translated his fine club form to the Test stage. Joseph scored a superb try at the Millennium Stadium, beating three Welsh defenders with a magical mix of power and acceleration.

That try assured his selection for England's next match, against Italy at Twickenham, where Joseph cut loose with two long-range tries that left defenders trailing in his wake.

"We've always known he had it in him but he's doing it on a consistent basis now," said Attacking Skills Coach Mike Catt after the match. "He's taken his chance and taken it well. Where he is at mentally, his confidence is exceptionally high. That's credit to what Bath are doing. They're playing his type of game. He's started enjoying himself again."

Ireland kept out Joseph in the next round of the Championship, as Lancaster's side were narrowly beaten, but Scotland could not shackle him when they travelled to London for the Calcutta Cup. He unlocked the Scots' defence with a sublime break and sidestep for his fourth try of the RBS 6 Nations.

England concluded the Championship scoring seven tries in a 55-35 defeat of France at Twickenham, though Joseph was not among the scorers. It mattered little as his four tries confirmed him as the 2015 RBS 6 Nations Championship's top scorer, ahead of team-mates Ben Youngs and Jack Nowell and Wales pair George North and Rhys Webb.

It was a magnificent comeback after 19 months out of the national team and, on the eve of Rugby World Cup 2015, it proved a timely reminder of Joseph's priceless ability to pierce Test defences

He could of course reflect on his debut tournament with significant personal satisfaction but, a few weeks later, Joseph received further proof of the impact he had made when he scooped two major individual awards from the Rugby Players' Association. Joseph was the Players' Player of the Year, with Bath team-mate George Ford, Northampton's Samu Manoa, Sinoti Sinoti of Newcastle and Exeter's Thomas Waldrom on the shortlist. He also claimed the England Player of the Year, accolade ahead of Ford, Harlequins' Joe Marler and Saracens' Billy Vunipola.

"I'm enormously proud to have my name on two of the RPA's awards, especially given the immense quality amongst the other nominees," Joseph said. "It's an absolute pleasure to have received this level of recognition from my peers. As always, I would like to thank the people who've made this possible – my family and friends, team-mates, coaches and all the people who have pushed me to strive to achieve my absolute best."

As Rugby World Cup 2015 approaches, England wonder if Joseph has produced his very best in an England shirt. What is certain, however, is that he is now one of the most dangerous midfield runners in world rugby.

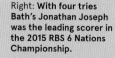

Right: **With four tries Bath's Jonathan Joseph was the leading scorer in the 2015 RBS 6 Nations Championship.**

IN THE SPOTLIGHT:

Stuart Lancaster

England
Rugby

Position: **Head coach**
Age: 45

The man charged with masterminding the England's bid to win Rugby World Cup 2015 on home soil, Stuart Lancaster's reign as head coach has seen a rejuvenated England develop into one of the most potent attacking Test teams in world rugby and genuine contenders to lift the Webb Ellis Trophy.

When the 45-year-old was appointed interim head coach ahead of the 2012 RBS 6 Nations Championship, English rugby was at a rather low ebb. The team's quarter-final loss to France at Rugby World Cup 2011 condemned them to an early exit from the tournament. England were now fifth in the World Rugby rankings, and optimism was in short supply.

Fast forward almost four years and the mood within the England camp could not be more contrasting. The team has been reborn under Lancaster's leadership and with a young and dynamic squad, hopes are high that England can be crowned world champions later this year.

By his own admission, England's transformation has been achieved as much by common sense as it has been by cutting-edge coaching techniques. One of Lancaster's first challenges was to reconnect the team with the supporters, and he admits the character of his players is as important as their ability.

"Players have to be humble, not to be arrogant, to respect each other and everyone else," Lancaster explained. "They have to accept the responsibility of being an England player. You've got to have character to be a great Test player. In a 50–50 selection decision, I'll always pick the player with the greater character. They also have to fit into the team ethic and what the team's all about. If a team isn't strong enough culturally then that can destroy a team."

After taking up the reins as coach, Lancaster invited former England players including Bill Beaumont, Peter Winterbottom and Will Carling to speak to the players about what it means to pull on the famous white shirt, and he also recruited the likes of former England footballer Gary Neville, rugby league internationals Kevin Sinfield and Jamie Peacock, ex-England cricket captain Andrew Strauss and Olympic gold medallist and Tour de France winning cyclist Sir Bradley Wiggins to address the squad and discuss how to create a world-class sporting environment.

The positive changes made by Lancaster off the pitch have been reflected in the side's performances on it. Their stunning 38-21 triumph over the All Blacks at Twickenham in 2012 was testament to the potential of the team and while England have come up just short in their four attempts at the RBS 6 Nations and the Grand Slam under Lancaster, clear progress has been made year on year.

England scored 18 tries in the 2015 RBS 6 Nations, their highest return for 12 years, and since Lancaster was appointed the team has played an exciting brand of rugby which has gone far beyond the side's traditional strengths in the forwards.

"You want a strong and physical set-piece so you can look to dominate up front," he said. "But also we want to play a style of

Stuart Lancaster's coaching career

2001–06	Leeds Carnegie, Academy Manager
2006–08	Leeds Carnegie, Director of Rugby
2008–11	Elite Player Development, RFU
2012–date	England Head Coach

rugby that excites the crowd and uses our talents. We've got some great footballers, some great ball-carriers, some power, some good distributors and, alongside that, we'd like our defensive system to be aggressive and give us opportunities to score tries by its effectiveness."

Lancaster's accent on youth has also played a major part in the reinvigoration of the team. When he announced his Rugby World Cup training squad in May this year, the average age of the group was 26, while there were 11 players among the 50 hopefuls under the age of 23.

His willingness to give youngsters their chance has seen the emergence of some of the most exciting English talent for years. With players such as Anthony Watson, Billy Vunipola, George Ford, Joe Launchbury,

Jack Nowell, Joe Marler and Jonathan Joseph, Lancaster has successfully nurtured a new generation of fearless Test stars.

His meticulous preparations for the 2015 Rugby World Cup have taken the head coach all over the world. Two years ago, he travelled to New Zealand and Australia, speaking with former All Black captain and coach Sir Brian Lochore, before visiting leading NRL (Australia Rugby League) clubs Sydney Roosters, Melbourne Storm and the South Sydney Rabbitohs in an attempt to further his own coaching education.

As the host nation, there will be huge expectations on England at the Rugby World Cup but the home faithful can be confident Lancaster has left no stone unturned in his bid to prepare the players for the challenges that lie ahead.

Below: **Stuart Lancaster's reign as head coach has seen England develop a more expansive and attacking style of play.**

England
Rugby

What's New at HQ

TWICKENHAM READY FOR GLOBAL GATHERING

When Rugby World Cup 2015 kick-offs in September at Twickenham, with the eagerly-anticipated opening game between England and Fiji, the stadium will proudly showcase the results of a major £76 million redevelopment.

The home of English rugby boasts more than a century of history, but time rarely stands still at HQ. Ahead of the 10 matches the stadium will stage during Rugby World Cup 2015, it has undergone a significant facelift to enhance its reputation as one of the greatest venues in world sport.

The Rugby Football Union began this work in 2012, when they laid a new state-of-the-art hybrid grass and artificial fibre pitch and, over the last three years, Twickenham has undergone a series of further upgrades and modifications designed to improve the match day experience for both spectators and players.

All three of England's Pool A games at Twickenham in Rugby World Cup 2015

are evening kick-offs and the pitch will be illuminated by the stadium's new LED floodlight system which was first employed in November 2014 for the visit of world champions New Zealand.

"We are one of the first stadiums in the world to have LED floodlights and as the nights draw in you will see these lights really come into their own,' said stadium director Richard Knight. "We have never before been able to provide such uniform lighting coverage of the pitch. The impact that they are going to have for spectators in the stadium, people watching the game on TV, players and referees is going to be a real game-changer. It will now be pretty much

Below: **Twickenham will host 10 matches – including the two semi-finals and the final – during this year's Rugby World Cup.**

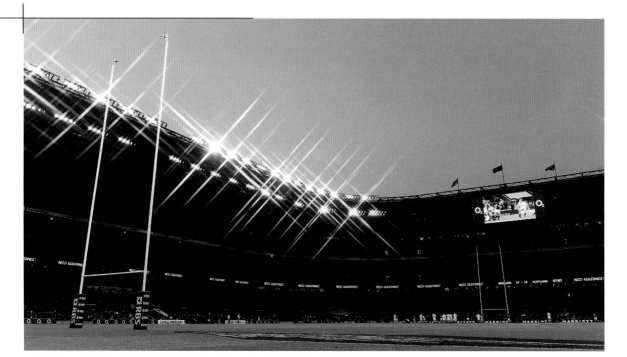

shadow-free because the lights are multi-directional."

The stadium now boasts two new giant screens at either end of the stadium, twice as large as their predecessors, and there is also a new PA system in place which can broadcast to up to 60 different areas of Twickenham simultaneously.

Spectators will gain entry through new electronic turnstiles that scan tickets and help reduce queues, while the RFU has doubled the stadium's wi-fi capacity to allow more fans to get online on match days. A total of 700 new digital screens have also been installed. Thirsty supporters will be able to wet their whistle at one of the 17 refurbished public bars in the stadium while one of the biggest jobs during the extensive redevelopment was replacing 26,700 seats.

The upgrades however have not been limited to areas of the stadium accessible to spectators. The medical facilities have been significantly modernised, with medics now able to study real-time video content on match days to better assess potentially serious injuries, while the media will benefit from a revamped and enlarged television gantry and a dedicated press conference facility for post-match interviews.

Twickenham's changing rooms have also undergone major changes, all supervised by men's head coach Stuart Lancaster. The new look is designed to emphasise the proud history of the team and it features a wall of honour with the name of every player to have been capped by England over the years. There is also a plaque above the pegs in the players' individual cubicles featuring a list of notable former internationals to have played in that position.

"We were looking at ways to strengthen the squad's identity and commitment, both to each other and our supporters, and the redevelopment of the changing room has an incredibly important role to play in this," Lancaster explained. "As well as the obvious design changes to improve the warm-up, coaching and analyst areas, we decided on a whole new look and feel for the space with an emphasis on celebrating the heritage of England rugby.

"We did this because we want the players to realise why they are playing and recognise those who have gone before them. This will help them to get that feel of camaraderie and honour of playing for England when they are pulling on the white shirt with the red rose."

Below: **The Twickenham changing rooms have been significantly remodelled to showcase England's proud rugby history.**

England
Rugby

Countdown to Rugby World Cup 2015

When World Rugby announced, in July 2009, that England would host the eighth edition of the Rugby World Cup, the countdown to the start of the game's most iconic showpiece event and the world's third biggest sporting spectacle began.

When the inaugural Rugby World Cup was staged in Australia and New Zealand in 1987, it marked a watershed moment in both the history and the expansion of the game. For the 16 competing nations, the tournament represented a step into the unknown and few could have predicted the fundamental impact the competition would have on rugby.

The success of the Rugby World Cup has been as revolutionary. The 2011 tournament in New Zealand attracted an estimated TV reach of 3.9 billion in 750 million households as the All Blacks were crowned world champions in Auckland and, as a result of the continued growth and ever increasing

popularity of the event, Rugby has never enjoyed a higher profile.

The massive logistical challenges presented by hosting Rugby World Cup 2015 have been the catalyst for six years of meticulous planning and preparation but with the tournament poised to finally begin later this year, the organisers believe the latest instalment of game's greatest global gathering will be the best yet.

"We are confident of a very special event that will capture the imagination on and off the field," said Bernard Lapasset, Rugby World Cup Limited Chairman. "Even before England and Fiji meet in the opening match

Left: **The Rugby Football Union's successful bid to host the Rugby World Cup in 2015 was confirmed by Bernard Lepasset six years ago.**

Above: **Newcastle United's St James' Park stadium will host three pool matches during the Rugby World Cup.**

on September 18, England 2015 will have raised the bar on several fronts, reflecting a sport that continues to grow at record pace around the world and the exceptional standard of organisation and delivery across all partners.

"From public sales to the official travel and hospitality programmes, we are anticipating record numbers, as fans from around the world join those across the UK in celebrating rugby and friendship.

"Across 44 days and 48 matches, the Rugby World Cup 2015 story will be told in more nations than ever before. Audiences in 207 territories will be inspired by new broadcast, social and digital innovations, while a record family of commercial partners will also project rugby to new audiences. All of this is great news for rugby worldwide as Rugby World Cup is the financial driving force behind the growth of the sport.

"A tournament of this scale and stature cannot be delivered without a shared vision and strong partnership and I would like to thank England Rugby 2015 and the Rugby Football Union for their continued focus on ensuring a superb event on and off the field. With final preparations well under way to welcome the world's top players representing 20 nations, the stage is set for a spectacular event that will engage and inspire audiences around the world."

First on the agenda for organisers after it was confirmed England would host the tournament for a second time, following Rugby World Cup 1991, was the selection of venues to stage the matches. A total of 13 were eventually chosen, from the Brighton Community Stadium on the south coast and Sandy Park, Exeter in the south-west, to St James' Park, the home of Newcastle United Football Club, in the north east. The geographical and atmospheric range of the stadia selected promise to deliver a superb stage for the eagerly anticipated celebration of rugby in 2015.

A wide range of accommodation and training venues in England and Wales –

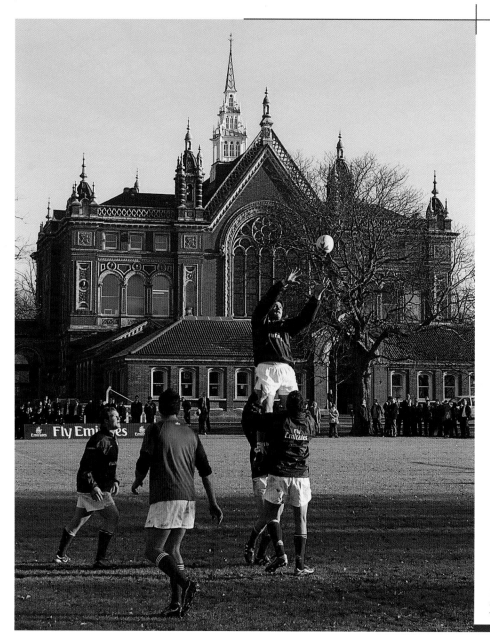

Left: **Dulwich College in London will be a training base for both Australia and Romania during this year's tournament.**

from the prestigious Celtic Manor Resort, near Newport, to Dulwich College, in south-east London – were also announced to cater for the 20 competing countries after a long assessment period, ensuring every team will enjoy unrivalled facilities as they fine tune their preparations for the competition.

"Players are at the heart of Rugby Cup 2015 and the facilities in stadia, at the training venues or team bases will be of an exceptional standard," said Head of Rugby

World Cup Alan Gilpin. "They will have everything they need to perform to their potential on the world's greatest rugby stage.

"It will be the same for fans from the in-stadia experience to Fanzones, broadcast and social media and we look forward to welcoming everyone in joining us to celebrate what promises to be an unforgettable and very special Rugby World Cup."

Spreading the rugby gospel far and wide has been a key element of the build-up

Above: **The Rugby World Cup Trophy Tour saw the Webb Ellis Cup visit 15 countries, including Canada, in the build-up to the tournament**

to the tournament and at the forefront of showcasing the game on the global stage has been The Trophy Tour, an epic worldwide journey which has seen the iconic Webb Ellis Cup visit a diverse range of communities in 15 different countries.

The international element of the tour began in May 2014, in Tokyo, and concluded 12 months later in Paris. On its remarkable travels the cup clocked up over 115,000 miles, stopped in 12 different time zones and crossed the equator six times. The countries it visited were Japan, Australia, Fiji, Madagascar, South Africa, Argentina, Uruguay, USA, UAE, China, Italy, Romania, Canada, Germany and France.

In total, the trophy visited 111 communities and involved more than 70,000 people in an international celebration of the game and was supported by appearances from 308 current and former Test stars from 27 different countries, including 11 former Rugby World Cup winners. France captain Serge Betsen, England's Will Greenwood and Australia's Nathan Sharp were just three of the legends to take part.

On the way, the Tour coincided with the play-off matches which confirmed the qualification of Japan, Fiji, Namibia and Uruguay for the tournament and also included a helicopter flight across the New York city skyline, a trip to the steps of the Sydney Opera House, a reception by the Royal Canadian Mounted Police in Toronto, and a visit to the iconic Burj Al Arab building in the UAE.

"The Trophy Tour has provided a further catalyst to the growth story and showcased our activities such as our Tackle Hunger partnership with the UN World Food Programme in Madagascar," said Bernard Lapasset. "It has been fantastic to see the tremendous reception that the Webb Ellis Cup has received along the way.

"Rugby is reaching out, engaging and inspiring new audiences around the world in record numbers. There are now more than 7.2 million men, women and children actively playing the sport and in 2014 alone 450,000 children were introduced to the game via World Rugby's Get Into Rugby programme."

Those globetrotting exploits however are far from the end of the Trophy Tour story and the Webb Ellis Cup will be proudly paraded throughout the UK and Ireland this year as build-up ahead of the Rugby World Cup reaches its climax.

The domestic leg of the 100-day tour began in Scotland on June 11 when the trophy visited Jed-Forest RFC in the Borders region. After five days in Scotland, it headed to Northern Ireland and then south to the Republic of Ireland before arriving for a 10-day journey across Wales. It will have travelled the length and breadth of England after that starting in Cornwall, culminating on the 100th day at Twickenham on September 18 for the Rugby World Cup opening ceremony and England's Pool A clash with Fiji.

"With more than 70,000 people celebrating

rugby in more than 100 communities across 15 countries, the Rugby World Cup Trophy Tour has been a great way for us to generate excitement around the globe during the build to Rugby World Cup 2015," said Stephen Brown, the Managing Director of England Rugby 2015.

"Young people and grassroots rugby were a key part of the Trophy Tour, helping to spread the reach of the game. Now the excitement will continue to spread as the Webb Ellis Cup embarks on a 100-day Trophy Tour around the UK and Ireland."

Supporters from home and abroad hoping to sample the unique atmosphere will not be disappointed and in March this year, England Rugby 2015 announced 15 Fanzones will be opened during the tournament, the first time in the history of the competition that every host venue, town or city would be supplemented by a dedicated area for fans.

Free to enter, the Fanzones will be open on match days and at varying times across the six-week tournament providing supporters with the opportunity to enjoy the build-up to matches and join in with the nationwide celebration of rugby. The Fanzone locations range from iconic town squares to city parks, match venue surroundings, and waterside spaces including the Docks in Gloucester and on the beach in Brighton. With capacities ranging from 2,000 to more than 10,000, and additional events planned outside of match days, more than one million fans are expected through the gates. All 13 Rugby World Cup venues will boast a nearby Fanzone with two additional supporter centres in Trafalgar Square, in central London, and in the town of Rugby, the world famous birthplace of the game.

Each Fanzone will include a big screen, with some showing live Rugby World Cup matches, grassroots and community rugby initiatives, food and drink, entertainment and unique regional content to celebrate the host city.

"Excitement is already building for this year's Rugby World Cup and the Fanzone is going to be the perfect place to take in the games and enjoy the festive atmosphere with like-minded sports fans," said Councillor Rosa Battle, Manchester City Council Executive Member for Culture and Leisure. "Boasting a selection of events across the weekend, the Fanzone is going to be a must-visit destination for everyone, whether they're going to the big game or just want to watch the match in style."

Fanzones however are only one part of the celebratory feel organisers are aiming to create during the tournament and, in January this year, England Rugby 2015 and the RFU unveiled their Festival of Rugby 2015, a programme which will see rugby themed events taking place across the UK.

The Festival of Rugby will provide clubs, schools, community groups, organisers of sporting events and the wider UK public with the opportunity to take part in the celebration of rugby in 2015 and create a true festival feel across the country. The Festival of Rugby is open to any event hosted between June 10 and October 31 that includes a rugby theme or element. This can be as simple as a link to a rugby team, song, food, visuals or cultural elements of the game

"We are delighted to be supporting and promoting the Festival of Rugby 2015 and look forward to engaging thousands of people across the country in rugby related activities, said Steve Grainger, the RFU's Rugby Development Director.

"Whether it's a playing opportunity for youngsters at a local community centre, a rugby themed music festival at a school or an exhibition of rugby artwork, the Festival of Rugby will demonstrate what a truly inclusive sport rugby is and will showcase the values of our sport. We're looking forward to seeing a wide range of projects in the Festival of Rugby, with the rugby family reaching out to more communities to welcome many more potential players, spectators and followers to our great game."

Another initiative from England Rugby 2015 to engage the younger generation in the upcoming tournament and the sport as a whole has been the selection of 20 school choirs from England and Wales to take part in the individual welcome ceremonies for the competing countries. More than 100 primary and secondary schools applied for the honour of singing at the events and after a difficult selection process conducted by England Rugby 2015, the Youth Sport Trust and the RFU, the list was finally whittled down to the lucky 20.

Right top: **Supporters will be able to gather at the Fanzone in Trafalgar Square, central London, to soak up the Rugby World Cup atmosphere.**

Right bottom: **A total of 15 Fanzones, up and down the country, will provide a focal point for fans during the tournament.**

"We were really pleased with the response we've seen from schools wanting to be part of the Welcome Ceremonies for Rugby World Cup 2015," said Stephen Brown.

"The standard of the applications was very high and I would like to thank all schools that took the time to apply. We now have 20 excellent choirs from across England and Wales that will help us to welcome the participating unions to the tournament and make it a celebration of rugby. We hope this will provide them with unforgettable memories and give them and the teams a fantastic tournament experience."

Stuart Lancaster's England team will be serenaded by pupils from Longcroft School in Beverley, East Yorkshire, when they are officially welcomed to the tournament in an event in London.

"Longcroft School is thrilled to be part of this prestigious international event," said head teacher Ian O'Donnell. "Alongside other successes, the school has a long history of both sporting and musical achievements, which makes welcoming the England rugby team all the more special. We are very proud of our Gospel Choir, which continues to go from strength to strength. Everyone at Longcroft wishes them luck and will be flying the flag for England, as they compete against other teams from around the world in Rugby World Cup 2015."

Rugby World Cup In Numbers

13	Venues selected to stage Rugby World Cup matches
20	Teams hoping to lift the Webb Ellis Trophy
40+	Bases chosen in England and Wales to host the teams
83	Nations who competed in the Rugby World Cup qualification programme
207	Territories to which the tournament will be broadcast
20,000	Hours of television coverage that will be shown
600+	Players who will be involved in the competition
48	Matches to be played
466,000	Estimated number of overseas supporters who will descend on England and Wales for the Rugby World Cup
2.3 million	Tickets for the tournament
1 billion	Extra pounds the Rugby World Cup will generate for the UK economy

Rugby World Cup 2015 Venues

Name	Venue	Capacity
Brighton Community Stadium	Brighton & Hove	30,750
Elland Road	Leeds	37,914
Kingsholm Stadium	Gloucester	16,500
Leicester City Stadium	Leicester	32,312
Manchester City Stadium	Manchester	47,800
Millennium Stadium	Cardiff	74,154
The Stadium, Queen Elizabeth Olympic Park	London	54,000
Sandy Park	Exeter,	12,300
St James' Park	Newcastle-upon-Tyne	52,409
Stadium MK	Milton Keynes	30,717
Twickenham	London	81,605
Villa Park	Birmingham	42,785
Wembley Stadium	London	90,000

Rugby World Cup 2015 Fanzones

Town	City Venue	Capacity
Birmingham	Eastside Park	8,000
Brighton & Hove	Madeira Drive	10,000
Cardiff	Cardiff Arms Park	5,000+
Exeter	Northernhay Gardens	5,000
Gloucester	Gloucester Docks	5,000
Leeds	Millennium Square	5,000
Leicester	Victoria Park	5,000+
London, Brent	Wembley Park	c15,000
London, Central	Trafalgar Square	5,000
London, Newham	Queen Elizabeth Olympic Park	c10,000
London, Richmond	Old Deer Park	10,000
Manchester	Albert Square	8,000
Milton Keynes	Campbell Park	5,000+
Newcastle-Upon-Tyne	Science Central	10,000
Rugby	Old Market Place	2,000

www.rugbyworldcup.com/fanzones

Festival of Rugby 2015

Rugby themed events are going to be taking place across the UK in 2015 as the nation prepares to celebrate what will be a massive year for the game. To get involved in the Festival of Rugby 2015, register your name and email address on this website **www.festivalofrugby2015.com**

Below: **Festival of Rugby events will be taking place around the UK in the run-up to Rugby World Cup 2015.**

England's Rugby World Cup Magic Moments

RUGBY WORLD CUP REWIND

Ahead of the eighth edition of the 2015 Rugby World Cup in England, we look back at eight of the men in white's greatest moments in the history of the tournament.

England 20   Australia 17 AET
(Final, RWC 2003)

Jonny Wilkinson registered a remarkable 36 drop goals during his record-breaking England career, but none were more important nor iconic as the glorious three-pointer he landed in Australia in the final of the Rugby World Cup in 2003.

England and Australia were deadlocked at 17-17 in extra-time after an epic tussle in Sydney. With less than two minutes to play, England's forwards rumbled forward deep into enemy territory. A break by scrum-half Matt Dawson and a crunching drive from skipper Martin Johnson made crucial metres and, as the pack secured ruck ball, the stage was set for the moment that redefined England Rugby.

The desperate Wallabies knew exactly what was coming but, as Dawson fired out his spiralling pass, there was nothing they could do but watch as Wilkinson took aim – albeit with his weaker right foot – and bisected the uprights. The game-clock showed there were only 28 seconds remaining, almost no time for Australia to reply.

England had one more task – claim the ball from the restart. They achieved this and when Mike Catt triumphantly hammered the ball into touch, the final whistle sounded meaning England had won the Rugby World Cup.

Right: **Jonny Wilkinson's extra-time drop goal sealed Rugby World Cup glory for England in Sydney in 2003.**

England 25   Australia 22 AET
(Quarter-Final, RWC 1995)

The Rugby World Cup 1995 quarter-final between England and Australia is remembered by many for Rob Andrew's dramatic winning drop goal in extra time, but it also saw the men in white conjure up one of the most spectacular tries in tournament history.

It came midway through the first half in Cape Town as Michael Lynagh spilled possession on the England 22. Andrew pounced on the loose ball before the Wallabies could react and he sent Jeremy Guscott racing upfield. As the Australian cover converged, Guscott found his midfield partner Will Carling, and the skipper, in turn, moved the ball wide to Tony Underwood on the right wing.

The Leicester flyer still had 50 metres to go, but he ignited the afterburners and despite a despairing, shoulder-high tackle from opposite number Damian Smith, Underwood had the pace and the momentum to get over the line for an irresistible counter-attacking score.

Andrew's drop goal may have actually decided the game, giving England a degree of redress after their loss to the Wallabies at Twickenham in the Rugby World Cup final four years earlier, but the three-quarter line's moment of magic allowed it to happen.

Below: **Wing Tony Underwood (left, celebrating with Mike Catt, centre, and skipper Will Carling) scored 13 tries for England, including a stunner against Australia in Cape Town in 1995.**

England 9   Scotland 6
(Semi-Final, RWC 1991)

There is rarely any middle ground for Test match kickers. A successful penalty, conversion or drop goal can create an instant hero of the hour, but a failure to bisect the uprights can suddenly condemn the player to the role of villain of the piece.

The Rugby World Cup 1991 semi-final at Murrayfield was a classic case in point as England and Scotland played out a cat-and-mouse encounter. A pair of Gavin Hastings penalties were cancelled out by two from Jon Webb to leave the score tied at 6-6 after 60 minutes. Scotland were then awarded a penalty in front of the England posts, 20 metres out, but full-back Gavin Hastings missed the simple kick.

England almost scored a try through Rory Underwood, but his pass to hooker Brian Moore was batted into touch by Finlay Calder a metre from the line. England forced a series of scrums until scrum-half Richard Hill passed to fly-half Rob Andrew, and his drop-goal sailed handsomely between the posts.

It sealed England's dramatic 9-6 victory and booked their place in the Rugby World Cup final. In addition, it helped to ease the pain of England's loss to Scotland in the 1990 Five Nations Championship Grand Slam decider at the same ground.

Below: **Fly-half Rob Andrew sent England through to the 1991 Rugby World Cup final with a late drop goal against Scotland.**

England 24　France 7
(Semi-Final, RWC 2003)

Many believe that losing a Rugby World Cup semi-final is more heartbreaking than to come up short in the final itself. Thus, thanks to the redoubtable and unceasingly reliable left foot of Jonny Wilkinson, England were spared that particular agony inside Sydney's Telstra Stadium in 2003.

France were England's opponents in the last four in Sydney, but torrential rain and high winds dashed any hopes of a free-flowing spectacle between the two sides, so England turned to Wilkinson to keep the scoreboard ticking over.

The fly-half responded superbly as he repeatedly punished French indiscipline and rewarded his pack for their muscular endeavour. Les Bleus were powerless to stem the flow of points.

In total, Wilkinson landed five penalties and three drop goals in a near faultless kicking display. Although France responded with a converted try from Serge Betsen, against the run of play, England defied the conditions to win 24-7.

The 24 points was Wilkinson's highest total in any Test in Australia. By adding 15 more in final, he finished with 113 overall and Rugby World Cup 2003's highest points-scorer.

Below: **Jonny Wilkinson's haul of 24 points was enough to beat France in the 2003 Rugby World Cup semi-final in Sydney.**

England 14　France 9
(Semi-Final, RWC 2007)

Josh Lewsey may have scored five tries in a Rugby World Cup match – the 111-13 defeat of Uruguay in Brisbane in 2003 – but his most memorable score came four years later when England faced France in the semi-finals in Paris.

The game was barely a minute old when scrum-half Andy Gomarsall unleashed a teasing box kick into the French 22. Full-back Damien Traille came across to deal with the danger, but he was undone by a cruel bounce. Traille then slipped and, as he looked up, Lewsey arrived on the scene like a runaway train. Lewsey gathered the ball and burst through Traille's despairing tackle to score.

The clock showed that just 78 seconds had elapsed when the try was scored and it turned out to be the only one of the match. Jonny Wilkinson and his opposite number Lionel Beauxis traded nine points apiece with the boot, so Lewsey's score proved the difference between in England's 14-9 victory.

Sadly, it was not all good news for Lewsey who limped off late in the first half at the Stade de France with a hamstring injury and thus missed the final. It proved to be both his final England try and the last of his 55 Test appearances for the men in white.

Below: **Josh Lewsey scored the only try as England edged out France in Paris in the 2007 Rugby World Cup semi-final.**

England 101   Tonga 10
(Pool Stage, RWC 1999)

A century of points remains a rarity in Test rugby and England have achieved it five times in their history, twice in the Rugby World Cup. The first time they recorded the feat in a Rugby World Cup match was in 1999 when they faced Tonga in the teams' final Pool B match at Twickenham.

It took England 12 minutes to breach Tonga's defence, when scrum-half Matt Dawson went over from close range. The Tongans drew level with a try of their own three minutes later, but the floodgates soon opened and England added another 12 tries, the first from hooker Phil Greening after 27 minutes.

The three-quarter line helped themselves to eight of those tries, with doubles for both wingers Dan Luger and Austin Healey and both centres Will Greenwood and Jeremy Guscot. Full-back Matt Perry chipped in with one as did hooker Phil Greening and flanker Richard Hill. Guscott's second try, in the final minute, was converted by Paul Grayson to give him a total of 36 points and to send England over the 100 mark. It was 36-10 at half-time but England took full toll on the Tongans – who were down to 14 men after prop Ngalu Taufo'ou was dismissed after 35 minutes. In all England scored 65 points in the second period.

Below: **Centre Jeremy Guscott was one of the eight England try-scorers against Tonga at Twickenham in 1999.**

England 60   Japan 7
(Pool Stage, RWC 1987)

Rugby World Cup 1987 – the inaugural tournament – was far from England's finest, but it was not without its moments to savour and the highlight probably was Mike Harrison's stunning display against Japan in Sydney.

England had suffered a disappointing 19-6 defeat against the joint-hosts Australia in their opening Pool One game a week earlier. However, any sense of gloom was soon dispelled at the Concord Oval as the Wakefield wing took full advantage of a Brave Blossoms defence unused to facing the quality England possessed.

The captain had scored his team's only try in the loss to the Wallabies, but he was in even more predatory form against Japan, scoring England's first Rugby World Cup hat-trick. Remarkably, his three-try salvo came in the space of just 13 minutes.

England ran in 10 tries in their 60-7 triumph, their first in the Rugby World Cup, and it laid the platform for the team to progress to the quarter-finals. The other try-scorers were: Rory Underwood, two, and one each for Nigel Redman, Gary Rees, Dean Richards, Jamie Salmon and Kevin Simms, while Jonathan Webb kicked seven conversions and two penalties.

Below: **Mike Harrison made history when he became the first England player to score a Rugby World Cup hat-trick in 1987.**

England
Rugby

England Expects

POOL A PREVIEW

Staging the Rugby World Cup affords Stuart Lancaster's team coveted home advantage throughout the tournament. However, being the host country also brings a weight of expectation which England must embrace as they bid to be crowned world champions for a second time.

When the draw for the Rugby World Cup 2015 was made three years ago, England found themselves in the same pool as both Australia and Wales. The consensus opinion was Pool A would prove the toughest in the tournament from which to qualify. England, therefore, would have to reach the quarter-finals the hard way.

The nation still expects and, as they prepare for action, the England team can look at their prospects in Pool A with an optimism borne out of their formidable record at Twickenham and a growing confidence strengthened by recent results.

Since the draw in December 2012, only New Zealand and South Africa have been victorious in the 16 Tests played at HQ, and neither the Wallabies nor Wales have been able to register a win on their most recent visits to south west London.

The last time England lost an RBS 6 Nations Championship match at the stadium was three years ago and their last competitive clash at the ground yielded a record half century of points as France were overwhelmed 55-35 in March.

Three of the England's four group games are at Twickenham – Lancaster's team will venture north for their final clash with Uruguay at the Manchester City Stadium – and if they top Pool A, their quarter-final, semi-final and Final will all be at

Below: **Home advantage and the England faithful will be crucial factors during the Rugby World Cup as Stuart Lancaster's team bids to lift the Webb Ellis Cup.**

Twickenham. By Lancaster's own admission, home advantage, and the roar of a capacity crowd, will be a potent weapon in his team's armoury.

England's Rugby World Cup record is a proud one. The only northern hemisphere side to win the Webb Ellis Cup after their triumph in 2003, England have never failed to reach the quarter-finals, and only the Australia, France and New Zealand can match their achievement of appearing in three finals.

History however will be forgotten when England kick-off against Fiji at Twickenham in the opening game of the Rugby World Cup 2015 and it will fall to the current generation of players to write a new chapter in the England Rugby record book.

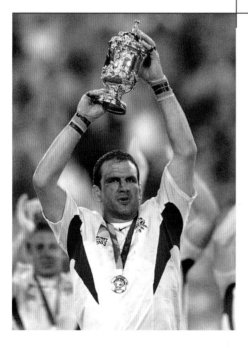

Below left: **Martin Johnson became a world champion in Sydney in 2003 after England's dramatic extra-time triumph over Australia.**

Below right: **England will play the first three of their Pool A fixtures of the 2015 Rugby World Cup in the familiar surroundings of Twickenham.**

Pool A Fixtures

18 September 2015	**England** v	Fiji	Twickenham
20 September 2015	Wales v	Uruguay	Millennium Stadium, Cardiff
23 September 2015	Australia v	Fiji	Millennium Stadium, Cardiff
26 September 2015	**England** v	Wales	Twickenham
27 September 2015	Australia v	Uruguay	Villa Park, Birmingham
1 October 2015	Wales v	Fiji	Millennium Stadium, Cardiff
3 October 2015	**England** v	Australia	Twickenham
6 October 2015	Fiji v	Uruguay	Stadium MK, Milton Keynes
10 October 2015	Australia v	Wales	Twickenham
10 October 2015	**England** v	Uruguay	Manchester City Stadium

England's World Cup Record

1987 – Quarter-finals	1999 – Quarter-finals	2011 – Quarter-finals
1991 – Runners-up	2003 – Champions	
1995 – Fourth place	2007 – Runners-up	

Scouting Report: Fiji

FIJI HOPES TO MATCH THEIR SEVENS FORM

The eagerly-anticipated opening game of the Rugby World Cup 2015, England's clash with Fiji at Twickenham, will be their sixth Test meeting. The faithful at HQ will expect a strong statement of intent from Stuart Lancaster's men at the start of the tournament, but England can ill-afford to underestimate the threat posed by John McKee's team.

It was on the Sevens circuit that Fiji first forged their reputation for a flamboyant brand of rugby that was as unpredictable as it was intoxicating. Fiji remain one of the game's great entertainers, and their ability to translate that instinctive style of play from the shortened format to the 15-man game will make them dangerous opponents in Pool A.

The Pacific Islanders booked their place at Rugby World Cup 2015 in typically effervescent fashion, despatching the Cook Islands 108-6 at the National Stadium in Suva in June 2014. The opposition may have been modest, but the 17 tries Fiji ran in, including a hat-trick from Nemani Nadolo, confirmed their fifth consecutive finals appearance in the Rugby World Cup, and seventh overall, spoke volumes about the attacking potential of the side.

"We knew the Cook Islands would come at us in the forwards in the first 20 minutes," Fiji captain Akapusi Qera said after the match. "We expected that, and we managed to compensate and come out with the win. It's a big thing for a rugby player growing up to qualify for the Rugby World cup and that's what motivated us in the second half."

The history of Anglo-Fijian games dates back to 1998, when Geoff Cooke's England team arrived in Suva after a two-Test tour of Australia and emerged 25-12 winners, thanks to two tries from wing Rory Underwood. England have won all four subsequent Tests, including a 45-24 victory at Twickenham in the pool phase of the 1999 World Cup. The latest meeting ended

> "It's a big thing for a rugby player growing up to qualify for the Rugby World Cup and that's what motivated us in the second half."
>
> **Akapusi Qera**

Above: Formidable Crusaders wing Nemani Nadolo will be one of the Pacific Islanders' most potent attacking weapons in the tournament this year.

Left: Fiji famously upset Wales in the pool stages of Rugby World Cup 2007 in France.

in a comprehensive 54-12 victory, also at Twickenham, in November 2012.

Fiji's recent record against their other Pool A opponents paints a mixed picture ahead of the tournament. Their stunning 38-34 victory over Wales in Nantes at the 2007 World Cup proved they were capable of taking the scalp of a top-flight nation on the big stage, and they drew 16-16 in a 2010 Autumn international at the Millennium Stadium, but Wales spectacularly exacted World Cup revenge in 2011 when they beat Fiji 66-0 in Hamilton. When the two teams renewed acquaintance at the Millennium Stadium in November 2014, Fiji came close to another upset before eventually losing 17-13 to Warren Gatland's team.

It has been 61 years, however, since Fiji recorded their last (and only second ever) win over Australia, while their clash with Uruguay at Stadium MK will be a repeat of the first and only Test between the two, back in 1999, a match the Fijians won 39-24.

Fiji have made solid strides forward since John McKee, a New Zealander who has previously worked with the Tonga national team, was appointed head coach in January 2014. His first game in charge, in June, saw a 25-15 victory over Italy in Suva. The Fijians were the top try scorers in the Pacific Islands Conference of the 2014 Pacific Nations Cup.

Like his predecessors, McKee's greatest challenge is bringing together a disparate group of players from clubs scattered across the world and successfully moulding them into a cohesive unit but there's no question he has talent at his disposal.

Giant Crusaders wing Nadolo, the joint top try scorer in Super Rugby in 2014, is perhaps the biggest name in the squad, but McKee can also call on the services of Leicester centre Verenki Goneva and Montpellier full-back Timoci Nagusa, while in the pack he has Glasgow Warriors second row Leone Nakarawa, his captain Qera and Brive flanker Dominiko Waqaniburotu.

Fiji reached the quarter-finals of the World Cup, in 1987 and 2007 – as well as the quarter-final play-off stage in 1999 – and if McKee is blessed with a full squad for this year's tournament, the Fijians will harbour hopes of a third appearance in the last eight.

Fiji's World Cup Record

1987 – Quarter-finals	2003 – Pool Stage
1991 – Pool Stage	2007 – Quarter-finals
1995 – Did Not Qualify	2011 – Pool Stage
1999 – Quarter-final play-off	

England
Rugby

Scouting Report: Wales

LOOKING FOR THEIR FIRST FINAL

The first and only northern hemisphere match in Pool A, England's meeting with Wales at Twickenham will be one both sides can ill afford to lose at such an early stage in the tournament. Wales reached the semi-finals in New Zealand four years ago, and look set to unleash a remarkably familiar looking side at this year's tournament.

The end of a World Cup cycle normally proves the catalyst for the overhaul of a team. Some players retire from Test rugby; others are no longer selected; and coaches often are replaced in the name of reinvention and rebirth as the build up to the next tournament begins.

Wales are an exception to this rule. Ten of the 15 who started their semi-final in Auckland against France in 2011 remain central to head coach Warren Gatland's current plans and whatever the exact complexion of the side selected to face England at HQ in September, it will be one brimming with Rugby World Cup experience.

Since the tournament four years ago, Wales have claimed two RBS 6 Nations titles – including the Grand Slam in 2012 – with essentially the same team and although they were denied the Championship this year on points difference by champions Ireland and runners-up England, the degree of continuity in selection afforded to Gatland makes his side a serious force.

They underlined that potential in November with a 12-6 victory over South Africa in Cardiff, a result secured by the metronomic accuracy of full-back Leigh Halfpenny's boot, the muscular midfield partnership of Jamie Roberts and Jonathan Davies and the settled backrow combination

Left: **Wing George North scored three tries for Wales at the 2011 Rugby Cup in New Zealand as Warren Gatland's team reached the semi-finals.**

Right: **Head coach Warren Gatland has presided over Wales' last two Rugby World Cup campaigns.**

of Dan Lydiate, captain Sam Warburton and Taulupe Faletau. Northampton wing George North missed the match, the win ending a 16-match losing sequence against South Africa, but the 23-year-old signed off in this year's RBS 6 Nations with a hat-trick against Italy in Rome to reinforce his reputation as one of the game's most potent finishers.

It has been 12 years since the last Anglo-Welsh showdown in Rugby World Cup, a quarter-final clash in Brisbane which Sir Clive Woodward's side won 28-17 thanks to 23 points from Johnny Wilkinson. Their only other World Cup meeting came at the same stage of the inaugural tournament in 1987, and also in Brisbane, when Wales were comfortable 16-3 victors.

The recent head-to-head record between the old rivals suggests a see-saw encounter at Twickenham. England have beaten Wales in their two most recent Tests, but Gatland's team registered a hat-trick of wins between 2011 and 2013. Significantly in the 10 meetings since the New Zealander was appointed head coach in 2007, the spoils have been shared, with five victories apiece.

In stark contrast Wales's record against fellow Pool A opponents Australia makes for sobering reading, with 10 successive losses to the Wallabies since a 21-18 victory in Cardiff in November 2008. However, as all of the five most recent defeats have been by five points or less, if Wales can discover the secret of getting over the line against the Australians, it could determine their fate in the group.

The Welsh will face Fiji at the Millennium Stadium in their third game in Pool A and history suggests a certain sense of trepidation throughout the Principality ahead of kick-off. Although Wales steamrolled the Fijians at the 2011 World Cup, running in nine tries in a 66-0 thrashing in Hamilton, Welsh supporters will not have forgotten a humiliating 38-34 defeat to them at the 2007 World Cup in Nantes. It was the upset of the tournament and it condemned Wales to a pool-stage exit.

The two sides last met at the Millennium Stadium in November 2014. Wales won 17-13 but Fiji played most of the second half with 14 men after prop Campese Ma'afu was shown a red card. The narrow margin of victory, despite their numerical advantage, leaves Gatland and his squad with food for thought ahead of the rematch at the Millennium Stadium.

Wales's opening game in the group is against Uruguay, the first ever Test against the South Americans and a loss to Los Teros in Cardiff would eclipse the Fiji result in 2007 in terms of shock value.

> "We are following the same methods that we implemented in 2011. That worked exceptionally well for us as regards our emphasis on fitness and conditioning."

Warren Gatland

Wales' World Cup Record

1987 – Third place	2003 – Quarter-finals
1991 – Pool Stage	2007 – Pool Stage
1995 – Pool Stage	2011 – Fourth place
1999 – Quarter-finals	

Scouting Report: Australia

England Rugby

ANOTHER DAY OF DESTINY WITH ENGLAND

A repeat of the Rugby World Cup finals of 1991 and 2003, A rematch between England and Australia at Twickenham in early October is potentially the defining game of Pool A. Recent history suggests an England victory, but with a new head coach in place and a mercurial attacking game at their disposal, the double champions will be nothing if not dangerous opponents.

There is a certain inevitability about an Anglo-Australian encounter at the Rugby World Cup. These old foes have met five times in the seven tournaments and although the most recent showdown was eight years ago – when Jonny Wilkinson kicked England to victory in the quarter-final in Marseille – the two teams are well acquainted when it comes to the business of vying for the Webb Ellis Cup.

The Wallabies won the first two Rugby World Cup meetings – including the victory over Geoff Cooke's team 12-6 in the 1991 Final at Twickenham – but England have won the three most recent World Cup contests, with their extra-time triumph in Sydney in the 2003 Final the defining moment in the England Rugby history.

That, however, is history, and as the two teams prepare to cross swords for a sixth time in the tournament, Australia are a team with a lot to prove but little to lose. Their preparation has been far from perfect. In October 2014, in the wake of a Bledisloe Cup defeat to the All Blacks, head coach Ewen McKenzie abruptly resigned. This followed a disappointing Rugby Championship campaign, in which Australia finished a distant third behind New Zealand and South Africa, and an increasingly fractious relationship with the media.

Three days later, Michael Chieka was unveiled as McKenzie's successor and although his credentials were impeccable, having led the Waratahs to a maiden Super Rugby title in 2014 – and Leinster to the Heineken Cup five years earlier – his appointment just 11 months before the start of the Rugby World Cup was certainly not how the ARU would have scripted the team's build-up.

Cheika's first assignment was Australia's end-of-season tour of Europe and although his reign began encouragingly with a 10th consecutive defeat of Wales in Cardiff, they subsequently slipped to narrow defeats against France in Paris, Ireland in Dublin and England at Twickenham to underline the size of the task facing the new coach.

Below: Jonny Wilkinson's iconic extra-time drop goal settled the final of the 2003 Rugby World Cup against the Wallabies in England's favour.

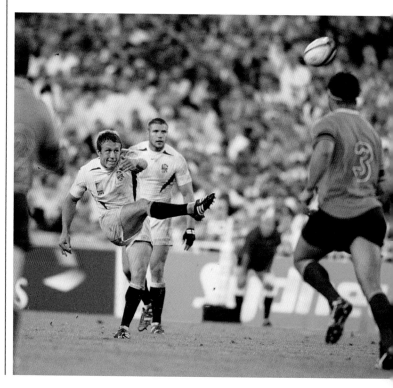

Australia's recent results against Stuart Lancaster's side will also be a source of concern for Chieka, who will combine the roles of Waratahs and Wallabies head coach in 2015. England have beaten the Australians in four of their last five meetings, most recently 26-17 at Twickenham in November courtesy of two tries from Ben Morgan.

The good news, irrespective of the outcome of the game against England, is that the Wallabies will be favourites to overcome the rest of Pool A. Their victorious sequence against Wales dates back to a 33-12 win at the Millennium Stadium in 2009.

Although they did suffer two shock defeats to the Fijians back in the 1950s, Australia have averaged more than 50 points per game in their last three clashes with the Pacific Islanders. Australia's match with Uruguay at Villa Park, Birmingham, will be a first meeting between them and Los Teros, but it is difficult to make a case for a South American triumph.

Australia have never failed to reach the quarter-finals of the Rugby World Cup, and their trump card is the team's ability with the ball in hand. Israel Folau, Adam Ashley-Cooper, Tevita Kuridrani and Christian Lealiifano are all world-class, while Chieka has successfully reintegrated potential match winner Kurtley Beale into the squad following his suspension last year for off-field indiscipline.

Consistency remains the Wallabies' Achilles heel, but their 12-12 draw with New Zealand in Sydney in August and their victory over South Africa in Perth the following month – and they are the two top-ranked teams in the world – are testament to Australia's potential and the danger they will pose to the other teams in Pool A.

> "England will be on home soil and the Welsh will be much closer to home than we will be. I'm sure they will be fancying their chances against us."

Michael Chieka

Australia's World Cup Record

1987 – Fourth place	2003 – Runners-up
1991 – Champions	2007 – Quarter-finals
1995 – Quarter-finals	2011 – Third place
1999 – Champions	

Right: **Australia's Israel Folau has scored three tries against Pool A opponents Wales in just two Test appearances.**

Scouting Report: Uruguay

England Rugby

LOOKING TO UPSET THE ODDS

Despite their status as the lowest ranked side in Pool A, the South Americans report for their third appearance at the Rugby World Cup this year hoping to upset the odds and reach the knockout stages for the first time in their history.

The last time Uruguay head coach Pablo Lemoine faced England at the World Cup, the 40-year-old was still playing in the front row, lining up for Los Teros in a pool stage encounter with in November 2003.

The former Bristol and Stade Francais tighthead scored Uruguay's only touchdown in Brisbane that day but, unfortunately for Los Teros, England replied with 17 tries of their own, including a record-breaking five from full-back Josh Lewsey. Clive Woodward's team mercilessly demolished the South Americans 111-13 en route to lifting the Webb Ellis Cup.

A dozen years on, and Uruguay will face England once again as overwhelming underdogs. After winning 48 caps, Lemoine now enjoys a less bruising life on the touchline but, whatever his personal memories he has of the rout in Brisbane, he is determined his current team make the most of their own Rugby World Cup experience in 2015.

"This is a huge day in our rugby history," he said after his side beat Russia 36-27 in Montevideo in October 2014 to secure their place in the finals. "It is one we must enjoy knowing that from now on the hard work will be with a clear goal, to enjoy the Rugby World Cup. We qualified because we wanted it more; we deserve it for all the hard work we put in the last four years and because, on the day, we managed to understand what was required to win."

Finalists in both 1999 and 2003, this Rugby World Cup will, nonetheless, be a journey into relatively unknown territory for Los Teros. That game with England in 2003 is the only meeting between the two countries, and they have played Fiji once before – losing in L'Aquila 16 years ago – but they have never faced either Wales or Australia at Test level.

Lemoine's side booked their place in the finals after going through the Repechage phase of the qualifying process. A 28-3

> "This is a huge day in our rugby history and one we must enjoy knowing that from now on the hard work will be with a clear goal."

Pablo Lemoine

Above: **Uruguay secured their qualification for Rugby World Cup 2015 after beating Russia 57–49 on aggregate in a play-off.**

Left: Rodrigo Capo Ortega has enjoyed a long career in European club rugby and he has been Uruguay's captain for almost a decade.

victory over Hong Kong at the Estadio Charrúa in August 2014 set up a two-legged showdown with the Russians.

Although Uruguay lost the away leg, 22–21 in Krasnoyarsk, second-half tries in the return, from centre Joaquin Prada, prop Alejo Corral and scrum-half Agustin Oramaechea, secured a 36-27 victory and a 57-49 aggregate triumph. They were the 20th and final team to book their place at this year's World Cup.

Uruguay's solid recent form saw Lemoine's side claim the South American Rugby Championship title in 2014, for the first time in 33 years, while the team also finished a respectable third in the Nations Cup staged in Bucharest later in the year.

Their performances at their two previous World Cups have also been encouraging given Uruguay's relatively modest playing resources and the perennial challenge of securing fixtures against the world's top teams. A 27-15 triumph over Spain in Galashiels in the 1999 Rugby World Cup ensured Los Teros did not return home winless in their first tournament and although their mauling by England four years later was a bitter pill to swallow, they did beat Georgia in Pool C in Sydney to register a second finals win.

The majority of Lemoine's squad are drawn from domestic leagues and nine of the starting XV which overcame Russia in the second leg of the play-off play their club rugby in Uruguay. The best represented team was the Carrasco Polo Club, based in the capital Montevideo, with three players – wings Santiago Gibernau and Jerónimo Etcheverry and prop Oscar Durán – all named in the team.

Three other members of that team – hooker and captain Nicolás Klappenbach, Corral and number eight Alejandro Nieto – are based in Argentina, while the remaining three are all with French clubs. Of those, Rodrigo Capó Ortega is the highest profile member of the current Los Teros squad. The veteran second row has more than a decade of Top 14 experience with Castres, while Ormaechea plays second division rugby in France with Stade Montois.

Uruguay's World Cup Record

1987 – Did Not Qualify	1999 – Pool Stage
1991 – Did Not Qualify	2003 – Pool Stage
1995 – Did Not Qualify	2007 – Did Not Qualify
	2011 – Did Not Qualify

England
Rugby

Scouting Report: Pool B

EVERYONE IS TRYING TO MATCH THE SPRINGBOKS

With double world champions South Africa the clear favourites to clinch top spot in Pool B, Vern Cotter's Scotland must ensure they do not suffer any slip-ups against Samoa, Japan and the USA if they are to join Heyneke Meyer's team in the knockout stages of the tournament.

On recent form, the current World Rugby rankings and reputation, the Springboks' progress to the quarter-finals appears a formality. Champions on home soil in 1995, and again in France eight years ago, South Africa are always an immensely physical force to be reckoned with, and it would rank as one of the biggest shocks in World Cup history should any of their Pool B opponents claim such a coveted scalp.

The only major cloud on the horizon for Meyer's side is the fitness of captain Jean de Villiers. The veteran Stormers centre dislocated his kneecap in November 2014 playing against Wales in Cardiff and, after surgery, it remains unclear whether the 34-year-old will recover in time to add to his tally of 106 caps and compete in a third World Cup finals.

Strength in depth is not a concern for South Africa, however, and even without De Villiers' reassuring presence, they remain the team to beat. Of the other teams in Pool B, only Scotland have beaten the Springboks. However, in 25 meetings, the Scots have emerged victorious only five times, most recently in 2010 – they were 21-17 winners at Murrayfield – but all the wins have been on home soil.

Since the arrival of Cotter as head coach in summer 2014, the Scots have experienced something of a revival, despite collecting the Wooden Spoon in the 2015 RBS 6 Nations Championship. Scotland failed to reach the last eight of the World Cup for the first time in 2011 – finishing third in their pool behind England and Argentina – and they will be desperate to atone for what was an unprecedented disappointment.

Scotland's Achilles heel in recent years has been a lack of tries, but Cotter has enjoyed some success in addressing that problem. The five tries his team scored in their 41-31 victory over Argentina in Edinburgh in November was the first time they had achieved that against top-ranked opposition in 15 years.

Below: **Scotland last beat South Arica at Murrayfield in 2010 and, overall, have won just five of the 25 meetings.**

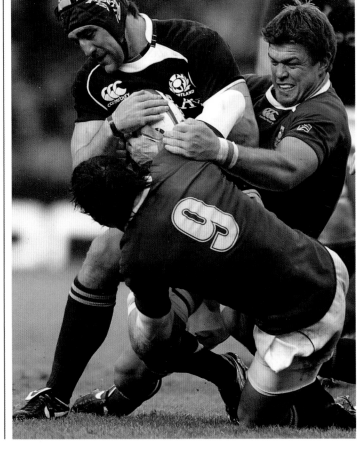

Right: **Rugby World Cup 2015 will be the first for South Africa head coach Heyneke Meyer after he succeeded Peter de Villiers in 2012.**

"You cannot be predictable. The game evolves every six months so we will try one or two new things."

Heyneke Meyer

The principal threat to Scottish hopes of making the quarter-finals will come from Samoa. The golden era of Samoan rugby was in the 1990s. They beat Wales in

Cardiff in both 1991 and 1999 and reached the quarter-finals in 1991 and 1995 – as well as the quarter-final play-off in 1999 – but the glory days are becoming a distant memory. Samoa's most recent World Cup quarter-final appearance was in 1995, but they won the Pacific Nations Cup Pacific Islands Conference title in 2014 and laid down a significant marker the last time they faced Scotland. The match was part of a quadrangular tournament, hosted by South Africa, in the summer of 2013 and, for the first time in nine meetings, the Samoans claimed a victory, 27-17 in Durban.

Japan boast a proud record of featuring in every World Cup since the inaugural tournament in 1987, but their return of one victory – a 52-8 defeat of Zimbabwe in 1999 – in 24 matches is less impressive and, having finished bottom of Pool A in New Zealand in 2011, the Brave Blossoms had to go through qualifying for a place in England this year. Coached by the former Wallabies head coach Eddie Jones, they achieved that by winning the Asian Five Nations title in 2014. As hosts of the next World Cup, Japan will primarily be looking to build the foundations of the team as 2019 beckons.

Appearing in their seventh World Cup, the USA also had to book their place in this year's finals and did so courtesy of an aggregate 59-40 win over Uruguay in a two-legged play-off.

The Eagles pushed both Ireland and Italy close in the group stage in the last tournament but have registered just three victories in 21 attempts in the finals and are the lowest ranked side in Pool B.

Pool B Fixtures

19 September 2015	South Africa	v	Japan	Brighton Community Stadium
20 September 2015	Samoa	v	USA	Brighton Community Stadium
23 September 2015	Scotland	v	Japan	Kingsholm, Gloucester
26 September 2015	South Africa	v	Samoa	Villa Park, Birmingham
27 September 2015	Scotland	v	USA	Elland Road, Leeds
03 October 2015	Samoa	v	Japan	Stadium MK, Milton Keynes
03 October 2015	South Africa	v	Scotland	St James' Park, Newcastle
07 October 2015	South Africa	v	USA	Olympic Stadium
10 October 2015	Samoa	v	Scotland	St James' Park, Newcastle
11 October 2015	USA	v	Japan	Kingsholm, Gloucester

Scouting Report: Pool C

England Rugby

ALL BLACKS WANT TO DEFEND THEIR CROWN

The defending champions, after their triumph on home soil in 2011, New Zealand's progress to the quarter-finals seems assured. The formbook suggests Argentina should also qualify from Pool C, but Tonga, Georgia and Namibia will all be hoping to upset Los Pumas' plans.

The aura of invincibility that envelops the current All Blacks team is rarely tarnished. In the 42 Tests they played between the start of 2012 and the end of 2014, they suffered defeat just twice and between their 38-21 loss to England at Twickenham in November 2012 and a 27-25 reverse against South Africa at Ellis Park in October last year, Steve Hansen's team went an incredible 22 games unbeaten.

New Zealand's consistency, since lifting the Webb Ellis Cup four years ago, has been simply phenomenal, and they have remained the number one ranked side throughout, as well as claiming a hat-trick of Rugby Championship titles in the process.

The All Blacks are also the only team in the history of the Rugby World Cup to have won every one of the 24 pool matches they have contested. Statistics can be misleading, but in this case, to predict anything other than a New Zealand procession in Pool C would be foolish.

The tournament looks set to be a last international hurrah for their captain Richie McCaw, 14 years after making his Test debut, and if the challenge of becoming the first country to successfully defend the World Cup was not motivation enough for the two-time champions, the imminent departure of their iconic skipper will surely galvanise them.

Whether it is the Argentineans who join New Zealand in the quarter-finals could hinge on their clash with Tonga at the Leicester City Stadium. They have never met at Test level but, based on the World Rugby rankings, it should decide who finishes second in the Pool.

The Pumas' recent Rugby World Cup

record is strong. Semi-finalists in 2007, eventually beating France in the third place play-off match in Paris, they once again made the knockout stages in New Zealand four years ago, succumbing to the hosts in Auckland in the last eight.

Since the last World Cup, Daniel Hourcade's side have experienced three seasons in the Rugby Championship and although they have finished bottom of the table each year, behind New Zealand, South Africa and Australia, their improvement was highlighted when they finally achieved their first win in the tournament in October last year when they beat the Wallabies 21-17 in Mendoza.

Tonga can only dream of such of a rarefied level of competition on such a regular basis and although they have never progressed from their group at a World Cup, their last two appearances in the tournament were nothing if not solid, beating Samoa and

Below: **Argentina made history when they beat Australia in Mendoza in October 2014, their first ever victory in the Rugby Championship.**

the USA in 2007 before famously upsetting France 19-14 in Wellington four years ago.

More significantly in terms of Pool C, however, was their recent clash with Georgia, a friendly in Tbilisi in November 2014, which 'Ikale Tahi won 23-9, courtesy of two tries from scrum-half Taniela Moa and a third from full-back Vunga Lilo.

The Georgians are making a fourth consecutive appearance at the Rugby World Cup and having finished fourth in Pool B in New Zealand in 2011, had to qualify for this year's tournament. They did so as the winners of the European Nations Cup Division 1A, ahead of Romania. With recent wins over Japan, Germany and Portugal, they will be hoping to register two victories in the pool stage for the first time.

Namibia are the other qualifiers and, having lost all 15 of their previous Rugby World Cup games since making their tournament debut in 1999, the Welwitschias will be focused primarily on trying to open their account in the competition. They are coached by their former Test prop Danie Vermeulen, and they secured their place in Pool C as the eventual winners of the Africa Cup, staged in Madagascar in the summer of 2014, edging out Zimbabwe on points difference in the final standings.

> "No side has ever won back-to-back Rugby World Cups. We will go in and try to win the competition."
>
> **Richie McCaw**

Pool C Fixtures

19 September 2015	Tonga	v	Georgia	Kingsholm, Gloucester
20 September 2015	New Zealand	v	Argentina	Wembley Stadium
24 September 2015	New Zealand	v	Namibia	Olympic Stadium
25 September 2015	Argentina	v	Georgia	Kingsholm, Gloucester
29 September 2015	Tonga	v	Namibia	Sandy Park, Exeter
2 October 2015	New Zealand	v	Georgia	Millennium Stadium, Cardiff
4 October 2015	Argentina	v	Tonga	Leicester City Stadium
7 October 2015	Namibia	v	Georgia	Sandy Park, Exeter
9 October 2015	New Zealand	v	Tonga	St James' Park, Newcastle
11 October 2015	Argentina	v	Namibia	Leicester City Stadium

Right: **The All Blacks are the defending Rugby World Cup champions after they narrowly beat France in the final in Auckland four years ago.**

Scouting Report: Pool D

England Rugby

FRANCE LOOK TO GO ONE STEP BETTER

A competitive pool, featuring three protagonists from the RBS 6 Nations Championship – Ireland, France and Italy – as well as Romania and Canada, all five teams have featured at every Rugby World Cup since the inaugural tournament 28 years ago.

The best team in the northern hemisphere, according to the World Rugby rankings, and the reigning RBS 6 Nations champions, Joe Schmidt's Ireland go into the World Cup as clear favourites to progress to the quarter-finals as Pool D winners and condemn the runners-up to a probable last-eight meeting with the All Blacks.

Optimism within the Irish camp is certainly justified. Their successful defence of the RBS 6 Nations this year came on the back of claiming the scalps of South Africa and Australia in the 2014 Autumn internationals in Dublin, while their recent, record 10-Test winning sequence which included victories over England, France and Italy in the RBS 6 Nations in 2015 will only have bolstered their growing confidence.

An abrasive back row and a world-class half-back pairing of Conor Murray and Johnny Sexton, coupled with Schmidt's tactical acumen, are Ireland's main strengths and, under the New Zealander's astute leadership, they have become a consistently tough nut to crack.

Their Rugby World Cup record, however, is modest. The only one of the Home Unions never to reach the semi-finals, Ireland have fallen at the quarter-final stage five times – most recently to Wales in Wellington four years ago – and Schmidt will make history if he is able to steer his team into the last four later this year.

The pivotal clash in Pool D promises to be its final fixture, when Ireland face France at the Millennium Stadium, their fourth meeting in the Rugby World Cup, and the French have won all three games – in a 2007 pool match in Paris and twice in the quarter-finals, in Durban in 1995 and in Melbourne in 2003.

Perennial bridesmaids, having lost in the Final three times, France's preparations for this year's competition have been at best chaotic. Head coach Philippe Saint-André, who steps down after the tournament, has had to endure a barrage of criticism from the media and supporters alike over his team's results and style of play.

Two wins in this year's RBS 6 Nations saw Les Bleus finish a disappointing fourth

Right: **After four years as France head coach, Philippe Saint-Andre will step down at the conclusion of Rugby World Cup 2015.**

Below left: **Ireland have lost to Italy just once since the inception of the Six Nations Championship in 2000.**

"I always say we've got to keep working on getting better because other people will be getting better."

Joe Schmidt

them to make an impact in the latter stages of this year's tournament.

Jacques Brunel's Italy avoided a second successive Wooden Spoon in this year's RBS 6 Nations Championship – they beat Scotland at Murrayfield – and the Azzurri will be hoping to qualify for their first quarter-final, after seven successive exits at the pool stages.

The Italians have won two and lost two in the pool phase at the last three Rugby World Cups but, with victories over both Ireland and France in the 2013 RBS 6 Nations Championship, they will harbour hopes of improving on that record.

Canada qualified for the Rugby World Cup after a 40-20 aggregate victory over neighbours the USA in a 2013 play-off, and the Canucks would welcome a repeat of their performance in the 1991 tournament, when they reached the quarter-finals, eventually falling 29-13 to New Zealand.

Coached by former All Black full-back Kieran Crowley, Canada have twice beaten Italy, drawn once with Ireland and beaten the French – albeit back in 1994 – but they have lost their last three Tests against Romania, most recently 18-9 in Bucharest in November 2014.

The Romanians, coached by former Wales assistant coach Lynn Howells, booked their place in the Rugby World Cup for an eighth consecutive time, courtesy of finishing second behind Georgia in the top division of the European Nations Cup. The Oaks will be looking to improve on their 2011 Rugby World Cup performance when they lost all four pool games.

in the table. Their heavy 55-35 defeat to England at Twickenham in their final game of the championship was France's 20th loss in 37 Tests since Saint-André's appointment after the 2011 Rugby World Cup, and it will require a dramatic reversal in fortunes for

Pool D Fixtures

19 September 2015	Ireland	v	Canada	Millennium Stadium, Cardiff
19 September 2015	France	v	Italy	Twickenham
23 September 2015	France	v	Romania	Olympic Stadium
26 September 2015	Italy	v	Canada	Elland Road, Leeds
27 September 2015	Ireland	v	Romania	Wembley Stadium
1 October 2015	France	v	Canada	Stadium MK, Milton Keynes
4 October 2015	Ireland	v	Italy	Olympic Stadium
6 October 2015	Canada	v	Romania	Leicester City Stadium
11 October 2015	Italy	v	Romania	Sandy Park, Exeter
11 October 2015	France	v	Ireland	Millennium Stadium, Cardiff

England line up ahead of the first Women's Six Nations Championship match of 2015.

ENGLAND'S WOMEN IN 2015

The Red Roses prepared for 2015 Women's Six Nations Championship acutely aware that their status as the reigning world champions would make them a prized scalp. England had undergone significant changes to their personnel both on the pitch and on the coaching side, and it was to prove a transitional campaign for the rebuilt squad.

England began their 2015 Women's Six Nations campaign with a trip to Swansea to face Wales.

2015 WOMEN'S SIX NATIONS

If England's triumph in the 2014 Women's Rugby World Cup was the result of years of continuity, 2015 was the year in which the Red Roses embraced a new era, with the advent of professionalism for their leading players.

More importantly, there were significant changes to the team's management structure. In late January, it was announced that Gary Street had parted company with England Rugby after seven successful years as head coach and that assistant coach Graham Smith would leave his position at the end of the championship.

Nicola Ponsford, Head of Women's Performance, was appointed interim head coach for the Women's Six Nations campaign while it was confirmed, four weeks later, that Simon Middleton would take a new dual role as head coach of both the 15-a-side and Sevens teams once the Women's Sevens World Series had finished in May.

The changes would have had a major impact at any time, but with the Red Roses also losing a number of their Rugby World Cup winners to Sevens duty for the first time in a bid to qualify for the 2016 Olympic Games in Brazil, there was a real sense of renewal within the England camp.

That England failed to claim a first Women's Six Nations title since 2012 was hardly surprising, but their performances in the tournament did signal the start of an exciting new phase for the side.

England
Rugby

Wales vs England

SHOCK AT ST HELEN'S

In the wake of England Women's Rugby World Cup glory in 2014, the 2015 edition of the Six Nations Championship saw England begin the process of overhauling their squad, but it was a case of evolution rather than revolution, starting with the Wales match in the opener at the St Helen's Ground in Swansea.

When Nicola Ponsford was confirmed as the interim head coach, she knew her first England team would bear little resemblance to the one that had beaten Canada in the World Cup final a few months earlier.

Six of the squad had already hung up their boots following the Red Roses' triumph. Seven more were absent, with leave, on Sevens duty in Brazil, but when Ponsford selected the squad to tackle Wales in early February, she was still able to name eight World Cup-winners, and there were just three new caps in the starting XV.

With regular captain Katy Mclean in Sao Paulo competing in the Women's Sevens World Series, Ponsford appointed Darlington Mowden Park Sharks' second row Tamara Taylor the new skipper, while the Test debutants were 19-year-old Bristol wing Sydney Gregson, club -mate Abigail Brown at centre and Richmond flanker Hannah Field. There was an experimental feel to the England bench with four uncapped players – Richmond's Victoria Cornborough, the Sharks' Abbie Scott, Worcester's Bianca Blackburn and Katie Mason of Bristol – included among the replacements.

"This season is the start of a new World Cup cycle for us," declared Ponsford before the match. "The Six Nations is an opportunity for us to bring on a number of new players. We have got some really exciting young players coming through who will learn a lot from this experience.

"Hannah, Abbie and Sydney have all played international sevens so they already have some experience under their belts. This talent will be supported by a huge amount of experience across the rest of the squad.

The pack is particularly strong, with players like Rochelle Clark, who knows better than anyone the intensity of Six Nations rugby, in particular playing away against Wales.

"I certainly think this year's Six Nations will be the most open yet. Everyone is going through a rebuilding stage after last year's World Cup but we are confident that we have a squad that can register a solid performance. We have had a really positive four-day camp together last week and we are all just eager to get started now."

The match at St Helen's was to prove an incredibly tight first-half contest as the two teams tested each other's resolve. A

Left: **Nicola Ponsford was appointed interim head coach of the England team.**

muscular run from Alexandra Matthews, followed by an incisive break by Darlington Mowden Park centre Ruth Laybourn, earned England a penalty chance, but Megan Goddard's kick fell short. The only score of the opening 40 minutes went to the home team, when wing Laurie Harries kicked a penalty on the stroke of half-time.

It was no less ferocious in the second half, but it was Wales who got what proved to be the pivotal first score when prop Catrin Edwards powered over from short range after 50 minutes. The conversion went wide, but the Red Roses now trailed by eight points.

The chance to reduce the arrears came in the shape of two Megan Goddard penalty attempts, but they were both off target. England's cause was not helped when scrum-half and vice-captain La Toya Mason was stretchered off with a leg injury. Although

Ponsford's team continued to ask questions of the Welsh defence, they were unable to make a breakthrough.

The final score also went to Wales. A pinpoint cross-field kick from fly-half Elinor Snowsill found Harries, and when she caught the ball and touched down, England knew their challenge was effectively over. This 13-0 win for Wales was only their second over the Red Roses, following a 16-15 success in the Six Nations Championship six years earlier, and a first defeat for England since being crowned world champions.

"We're obviously really disappointed by the result, but I have to give credit to Wales," Ponsford conceded after the final whistle.

"That's probably one of the best Welsh performances I've seen. They played really well today, they didn't allow us to create a platform and attack in the way we wanted to attack."

Right: **Sharks second row Tamara Taylor leads out the England team for the game against Wales at St Helen's.**

Far right: **Abbie Scott wins a lineout as England battled bravely in the Principality but, ultimately, they opened the Championship with a defeat against Wales.**

England
Rugby

England vs Italy

RETURN TO WINNING WAYS

Stung by the defeat in Wales, England regrouped ahead of their next match in the Championship – Italy at the Twickenham Stoop. And the team was bolstered by the return of a reassuringly familiar face to the fold.

Talismanic is an adjective diminished by its overuse in sport but, in the case of Katy Mclean, it could not be more fitting. The absence of the World Cup-winning captain for the team's Six Nations opener in Wales was keenly felt and Nicola Ponsford was able to recall the fly-half for the match against the Azzurri.

The return of Mclean, who was named vice-captain with Tamara Taylor remaining captain, was one of the five changes to the team beaten in Swansea. Hooker Victoria Fleetwood and scrum-half Bianca Blackburn were drafted in to replace the injured pair of Emma Croker and La Toya Mason, while second row Abbie Scott was handed her first Test start. The other change was at number 8, with Harriet Millar-Mills starting. In a remodelled back row, Alex Matthews moved to blindside flanker, while Hannah Gallagher remained as openside.

"There are a number of changes to the starting line-up and that is because of a handful of players putting their hands up for selection after good starts from the bench against Wales, or because of injuries," Ponsford said. "With Katy Mclean starting, she will bring experience and solidity to the midfield, which will allow us to control the game better than we did last week.

"We certainly know the areas we need to improve on, like being more clinical and

Left: **Kay Wilson can't be stopped as she goes over the line to score England's sixth and final try against Italy.**

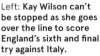

Right: **Fly-half Katy Mclean returned to the England team after being on Sevens duty with the Red Roses in Brazil.**

Far right: **Flanker Hannah Gallagher is all smiles as she is congratulated after scoring a long-range try.**

sticking to the game plan. Italy always keep going for the full 80 minutes. They work very hard and they are a very physical side at the breakdown, where they will try and disrupt our play."

England had been shut out in the defeat to Wales, but it took Mclean a mere three minutes to address that shortcoming against Italy, stroking over an early penalty to settle any lingering Red Roses nerves.

The converted try from second row Flavia Severin to give the Azzurri a 7-3 advantage was not in the script, but they were not in front for long as a powerful run from Matthews resulted in England's first try. Mclean made no mistake with the conversion to extend a lead the Red Roses would not relinquish.

England scored their second try moments before half time, when Scott celebrated her first international start with a maiden Test try. As the two teams headed to the changing rooms, the reigning world champions could reflect on a vastly improved display in the opening 40 minutes.

Italy's cause was not helped soon after the break when fly-half Beatrice Rigonni was shown a yellow card after a series of Azzurri infringements. England eventually punished their indiscipline after good hands from Sarah McKenna and Abigail Brown created space for Ceri Large. Mclean

successfully added the extra two points and the Red Roses were 22-7 ahead.

The fourth England try was a result of speed of thought, rather than speed of foot, as Mclean took a quick tap penalty from five metres out.

An eye-catching long range effort from Gallagher, brought a fifth try. The openside flanker sliced through the Italian defence and then showed the covering defence a clean pair of heels to touch down in the corner. Substitute Megan Goddard knocked over the conversion from the touchline and England were effectively out of sight.

There was still time for a sixth and final try, and it went to full-back Kay Wilson with the final play of the match to wrap up a comfortable 39-7 triumph. It went a long way to erasing the memories of the side's disappointment the previous weekend.

"The first half was frustrating but all credit to Italy," Mclean said after her 12-point contribution at the Stoop. "We had so much possession, and we just didn't make enough clinical decisions.

"But it's a new squad. I've got about six caps less than the whole back line put together. I don't think you can hide away from the fact that these girls are going on to play in the next Rugby World Cup, but that's in three years time, and this is a massive learning curve."

England
Rugby

Ireland vs England

REVENGE FOR IRELAND

Just six months after the two sides had met in the semi-final of the Women's Rugby World Cup in France, the Red Roses prepared to tackle Ireland again, aiming to repeat the victory they had registered in Paris in 2014. This time the match was at Ashbourne RFC, north of Dublin

With England's Women's Six Nations account open, and confidence restored after beating Italy, interim head coach Nicola Ponsford named her squad to face Ireland. Continuity and consistency were at the forefront of her thinking, so it was little surprise that there were just three changes to the matchday 23 and one in the starting XV, when the squad was announced.

That change in the run-on XV saw Saracens full-back Lauren Cattell replace Kay Wilson, who was on Sevens duty, to win her 10th cap. On the bench, Bristol centre Amber Reed returned after injury, while there was also a call-up for uncapped Darlington Mowden Park Sharks prop Heather Kerr. There was, however, a change in the captaincy as Tamara Taylor stepped aside to allow Katy Mclean to regain the honour.

"Without doubt playing Ireland will be the toughest game of the Six Nations so far for us," Ponsford admitted. "They are a well-drilled and physical side. We have learned our lessons from our loss in Ireland two years ago, so we will be ready to take on this challenge.

"We started this campaign with a significant number of new players in this squad, with the focus on giving them the opportunity to develop at this level. We want to be as consistent as we can with selection throughout the Six Nations, so we have only made one change to the starting line-up."

The blustery conditions made sustained periods of fluent rugby a near impossibility as both teams made an uncharacteristically high number of handling errors, but it was

Left: It was a night of frustration for England as Ireland ran out narrow 11–8 victors in their Women's Six Nations clash

Top: **England on the attack as they valiantly try to break down the solid Irish defence.**

Above: **Hannah Gallagher tries an unusual technique to stop Ireland's Jenny Murphy at Ashbourne RFC.**

England who opened the scoring after number eight Harriet Millar-Mills was high-tackled and Mclean stepped forward to bisect the posts with the resulting penalty.

Ireland full-back and captain Niamh Briggs levelled matters for the hosts with a penalty, but the Red Roses hit back shortly before half time with a close-range try. Mclean was initially held up short, but England were awarded the feed at the scrum by American referee Leah Berard.

After a clean strike from hooker Victoria Fleetwood, the pack rumbled forward with irresistible momentum. It was left to Millar-Mills to control the ball expertly at her feet before dropping on it for the try. Mclean was off-target with the conversion, but England headed to the dressing room with an 8-3 lead.

The second half was as attritional as the first, but Ireland struck first. Leinster scrum-half Larissa Muldoon took a quick tap penalty deep in England territory and darted over the line. Although Briggs was unable to add the conversion, the try levelled the scores at 8-8.

It looked increasingly as though the next score would prove decisive and, disappointingly, it went to the home side. With just six minutes left on the clock, a series of Ireland drives took them into the England 22 and with the defence creaking the pressure finally told. The Red Roses were penalised for coming in at the side of the ruck directly in front of their posts. Despite the powerful breeze, Briggs made no mistake with her kick.

Leading 11-8, Ireland had only a few minutes to withstand England's final throw of the dice, and they successfully held firm to condemn Ponsford's side to their second defeat of the Championship.

"The wind was incredibly difficult to deal with, but they probably played the conditions better than we did," Ponsford said. "It really disrupted our passing and handling. This side has come a long way from the Wales performance in our opening game and we managed to put together a lot more passages of play.

"But I am really pleased with the way the girls dug in to survive when Ireland were driving forwards five or six times and we put into practice what we have been working on."

England
Rugby

England vs Scotland

LAYBOURN'S HAT-TRICK HEROICS

Despite two defeats in their opening three games, the Red Roses regrouped ahead of the penultimate round of Six Nations fixtures knowing victory over Scotland in Darlington would reignite their hopes of clinching the Championship title.

Injuries are a cruel occupational hazard in elite sport and when Nicola Ponsford named her team to face Scotland at the Northern Echo Arena, the interim head coach finally had good news for two players who had suffered prolonged and frustrating spells on the sidelines.

Worcester wing Lydia Thompson hadn't played for England since the side's game group game against Spain in the Rugby World Cup in August, while Richmond full-back Fiona Pocock's last Test had come against Ireland in the 2013 Women's Six Nations Championship, but both were restored to the side to face Scotland.

Their recalls were two of five changes to the matchday squad, with Lichfield prop Justine Lucas and Richmond second row Rowena Burnfield replacing Laura Keates and Abigial Scott in the starting XV, while Saracens flanker Hannah Field took Hannah Gallagher's place among the replacements.

"It's great to welcome Lydia and Fiona back into the squad after their absence through injury," Ponsford said. "Both are quality players who have proved themselves on the world stage at both the 2014 and 2010 Rugby World Cups. They are now ready to come back into the mix and I am really

Left: Lydia Thompson dives over the line between the uprights after her mazy run had bamboozled the Scotland defence.

The half-hour mark saw England breach the Scottish defence for a third time, Lucas the player to touch down after a destructive rolling maul from the Red Roses pack. Just before half-time, veteran front row Rochelle Clark scored from close range after another powerful drive from her fellow forwards. It was her 21st try for her country in her 99th Test appearance.

England were 20-6 to the good at half time and they ensured Scotland remained on the back foot with the first score of the second 40 period, Pocock celebrating her return to international rugby with a simple try that owed much to some muscular preparatory work from substitute hooker Amy Cokayne.

The visitors briefly rallied with Scotland's first try on English soil for seven years when wing Eilidh Sinclair pounced on a loose ball after a misplaced England pass inside their own 22 to sprint over. England refused to be rattled by the surprise score and there were to be three more tries for the home fans to cheer.

An incisive break from Mclean paved the way for Laybourn's second. She was hauled down five metres short of the line, but as the Scottish defensive line back-pedalled furiously, Laybourn had the simplest of tasks to touch down in the corner.

The Red Roses' penultimate try was a dazzling solo effort from Thompson, on her Test comeback, carving through the opposition with a blistering burst of pace. The final word fittingly belonged to the irrepressible Laybourn, who raced over to complete her hat-trick and register England's eighth try of the game.

This resounding 42-13 victory ensured the Red Roses would go into the final round of matches in the Championship the following weekend still with the chance to lift the trophy, albeit relying on other results. Although she had an uncharacteristically wayward match with the boot, missing six conversion attempts, Mclean was delighted with the position the side had put themselves into.

"To be honest I'm probably disappointed with my own performance, but as a team we were better," the captain said. "We still weren't brilliant, but the beauty of the Six Nations is that we get to play next weekend against France at Twickenham."

Top: **Fiona Pocock celebrated her first Red Roses start for two years with a try in the right corner.**

Above: **Scotland replacement Jenny Maxwell arrives too late to stop Ruth Laybourn completing her hat-trick of tries in Darlington.**

looking forward to seeing them back in an England shirt."

After their disappointment against Ireland a fortnight earlier, it was vital England started brightly, and they did exactly that. In the opening 60 seconds, the Red Roses worked an early overlap for wing Ruth Laybourn, appearing on her home ground, and she scored in the right-hand corner.

A second score soon followed when captain Katy Mclean asked questions of the defence to create the space for lock Tamara Taylor to crash over. Although centre Nuala Deans kicked two successful penalties to open Scotland's account, England already were firmly in control of the match and they refused to let their intensity diminish.

England vs France

CLARK'S MAGNIFICENT CENTURY

With the destination of the title out of their own hands, England welcomed France to Twickenham more in hope than expectation of being crowned champions but, regardless of the result, it was a match with huge resonance for the longest-serving member of the Red Roses squad.

To represent your country just once is a considerable achievement. To make 100 appearances at Test level is simply phenomenal and, before England played at HQ, just one woman – hooker Amy Garnett - had reached the fabled milestone of a century of caps for the Red Roses.

The exclusive club of one became two in March when Nicola Ponsford announced her team to face the French and the name of Rochelle Clark was on the team sheet, confirmation that, 12 years after making her England debut against Canada in 2003, the 33-year-old World Cup-winner would also become a Test centurion.

"There might be a few tears, knowing me," Clark admitted before the game. "I'm going to be overwhelmed with pride and passion. Being out there will be one of the best feelings in the world. The game has massively changed since I got my first cap. It's much more professional, more physical, more powerful, and the players are getting stronger and faster all the time. But I'm playing some of my best rugby and really enjoying it.

"The French pack is really strong. They are a very good mauling side, so it's key that we keep our discipline and don't give away silly penalties so they can maul from the resulting lineouts. And they've got some exciting, fast backs that we need to take care of. It's going to be a tough game but our young side is getting better all the time."

Far left: **Record-breaking Rochelle Clark salutes the Twickenham crowd on the day she won her 100th cap for the Red Roses.**

Left: **Amber Reed kicked a penalty and a conversion in England's narrow 15–21 reverse against the French at Twickenham.**

Those England youngsters were under no illusions what they had to do to win the championship before kick-off. France had to be defeated by 10 clear points at Twickenham and then they had to hope for an improbable Scotland victory over Ireland in Cumbernauld 24 hours later.

France had secured the Grand Slam in 2014 and they showed their class in the early exchanges, with a penalty from full-back Jessy Tremouliere. A 21st-minute try from hooker and captain Gaelle Minot after a trademark rolling maul to established a 10-0 advantage. Tremouliere's second penalty extended the French lead, but England were on the scoreboard when centre Amber Reed was on target with a penalty, so the Red Roses found themselves 13-3 adrift at half-time.

A third Tremouliere penalty soon after the resumption further stretched the lead, but the first try of the half went to England, on 60 minutes, when flanker Hannah Gallagher was on hand to take a scoring pass from prop Laura Keates. Reed could not add the conversion, but the difference was now down to eight points with a quarter of the match remaining. England had to score next, but the ubiquitous Tremouliere scored a third French try to make it 21-8.

The Red Roses' fleeting hopes of winning the title had evaporated, but England finished with a flourish in front of their own supporters. A series of drives from the pack in the French 22 resulted in a try for substitute Harrier Millar-Mills, her second of the tournament. Reed added the conversion and, at the final whistle, it was 21-15 to the visitors.

France's victory was not enough to retain their title because Ireland defeated Scotland the following day to top the table on points difference. Italy's suprise win over Wales saw them take third place ahead of England.

For a side boasting a Rugby World Cup in the trophy cabinet, fourth was a modest return for the campaign but Ponsford was confident the side were heading in the right direction nonetheless.

"We always knew that this Six Nations campaign was going to be difficult," she said after her last match as interim head coach, and the imminent arrival of Simon Middleton as Gary Street's permanent replacement. "We've had nine new caps but we've had a significant number of those playing well against France.

"That's the biggest bonus we've got out of this. I said to the players at the end, from where we were when we played the Wales game, I think we've made a step on every game that we've played and that's what we set out to do."

Right: **England were defeated at Twickenham despite a second-half fightback and tries from Hannah Gallagher and Harriet Millar-Mills.**

2015 Women's Six Nations Statistics

Results

8 FEBRUARY 2015 (ST HELEN'S, SWANSEA)

Wales 13   **England** 0

15 FEBRUARY 2015 (TWICKENHAM STOOP, LONDON)

England 39   **Italy** 7

27 FEBRUARY 2015 (ASHBOURNE, COUNTY MEATH)

Ireland 11   **England** 8

13 MARCH 2015 (NORTHERN ECHO ARENA, DARLINGTON)

England 42   **Scotland** 13

21 MARCH 2015 (TWICKENHAM)

England 15   **France** 21

Final Table

TEAM	P	W	D	L	F	A	PD	TRIES	PTS
Ireland	5	4	0	1	139	26	113	20	8
France	5	4	0	1	113	44	69	16	8
Italy	5	3	0	2	82	94	-12	13	6
England	5	2	0	3	104	65	39	17	4
Wales	5	2	0	3	64	73	-9	9	4
Scotland	5	0	0	5	27	227	-200	2	0

2015 Women's Six Nations Scorers

Katy **MCLEAN**	15 (1T, 2C, 2P)
Ruth **LAYBOURN**	15 (3T)
Hannah **GALLAGHER**	10 (2T)
Harriet **MILLAR-MILLS**	10 (2T)
Amber **REED**	7 (2C, 1P)
Alexandra **MATTHEWS**	5 (1T)
Abbie **SCOTT**	5 (1T)
Ceri **LARGE**	5 (1T)
Kay **WILSON**	5 (1T)
Tamara **TAYLOR**	5 (1T)
Justine **LUCAS**	5 (1T)
Rochelle **CLARK**	5 (1T)
Fiona **POCOCK**	5 (1T)
Lydia **THOMPSON**	5 (1T)
Megan **GODDARD**	2 (1C)

Right: **Alexandra Matthews was an ever-present for the Red Roses' during the Women's Six Nations, scoring one try.**

Championship Appearances

5	Rochelle **CLARK**	**3**	Hannah **FIELD**	**1**	Lauren **CATTELL**
	Ceri **LARGE**		Sydney **GREGSON**		Emma **CROCKER**
	Ruth **LAYBOURN**		Laura **KEATES**		Megan **GODDARD**
	Alexandra **MATTHEWS**		Harriet **MILLAR-MILLS**		La Toya **MASON**
	Tamara **TAYLOR**		Abbie **SCOTT**		Amber **REED**
4	Abigail **BROWN**	**2**	Rowena **BURNFIELD**		
	Bianca **BLACKBURN**		Justine **LUCAS**		
	Victoria **FLEETWOOD**		Fiona **POCOCK**		
	Hannah **GALLAGHER**		Lydia **THOMPSON**		
	Katy **MCLEAN**		Kay **WILSON**		

"I think we've made a step on every game that we've played and that's what we set out to do at the start of the tournament."

Nicola Ponsford

Above: **Fly-half Katy Mclean was England's joint-top scorer in the Women's Six Nations Championship with 15 points.**

IN PROFILE:

Rochelle Clark

England Rugby

Position: Openside prop
Age: 34
Height: 1.70m
Weight: 86kg
Caps: 100
Points: 105 (21T)

The rock on which the England pack is built, prop Rochelle Clark is still going strong after 12 bruising years of Test rugby for the Red Roses and despite lifting the Rugby World Cup last year, the 34-year-old insists she's still not ready to make way for her younger rivals.

For more than a decade, the durable Clark has taken everything the opposition can throw at her and come back for more. The Worcester prop could have retired after England's Women's Rugby World Cup triumph in Paris last August. It might have seemed a good time to call it a day, but her competitive instincts proved stronger than the discomfort of aching bones and she opted to continue her career.

The decision has reaped significant rewards for both Clark and for England. In December 2014, she was awarded an MBE in the Queen's New Year Honours List. And she was in vintage form in the 2015 Women's Six Nations, starting all five games as interim head coach Nicola Ponsford, used her match experience to help the young, transitional Red Roses squad.

In March, when England met France in the final match of the tournament at Twickenham, Clark won her 100th cap, and became only the second Englishwoman, after Amy Garnett, to reach the milestone. To honour it further, Clark led out the team before the match.

"It was the best feeling in the world to be honest," she said. "Obviously Amy has got 100 caps, and she has been a hero of mine ever since I was younger, so to be anywhere near her has been brilliant. I was just so honoured to run out at Twickenham and lead the team. It was a very emotional and overwhelming day.

"There were just so many messages of good luck and congratulations. There is no better honour than running on to the pitch in your white shirt with that red rose on your chest."

Two months later, there was further reason to celebrate when she was named *The Sunday Times* England Women's Player of the Year, emerging from a fiercely competitive shortlist featuring Tamara Taylor, Emily Scarratt and Alexandra Matthews to land the award.

Clark's journey to the pinnacle of the game began when, at the age of 15, she was persuaded to turn her back on basketball and take up rugby with Beaconsfield. The new sport proved very much to her liking and after graduating through the England Under-19 set-up and beyond Academy level, she was handed her senior Test debut by former coach Geoff Richards against Canada in Vancouver in the summer of 2003.

She appeared in the finals of the Women's Rugby World Cup in 2006 and 2010 before last year's victory in France, plus multiple Women's Six Nations titles, but Clark has also pursued outside interests away from the pressure of international rugby. She completed a degree in Sports Science & Coaching at the College of St Mark and St John in Plymouth and is currently filling the role of head coach for the both the Chesham Stags club and the Buckinghamshire University teams.

The England team, however, remains her first love and she is adamant she has the desire and stamina to be a mainstay of the Red Roses' bid to defend their Women Rugby World Cup crown in Ireland in 2017.

"There is nothing I can do about my age but I really want to help England win it again," she said. "I am playing some of the best rugby of my career, and Worcester are also playing well. So, as long as the coaches are still picking me, I am still as hungry as ever to keep fighting and make that number one shirt mine.

"My body is feeling good, so the plan is to carry on and hopefully defend our World Cup title. You're a long time retired. I still love the game. I still play as much as I can. I'm coaching all I can. Rugby is my life and I want to keep going as long as possible. I'm leaving the dream at the moment."

Right: **Rochelle Clark has been a stalwart of the England side since she made her debut against Canada in 2003.**

IN THE SPOTLIGHT:

Simon Middleton

England Rugby

Position: **Women's head coach**

Age: **49**

Appointed coach of the England Women's 15-a-side and Sevens squads in February 2015, Simon Middleton is a man with a busy schedule as he aims to take the Red Roses forward on two fronts.

To follow in the footsteps of a coach who has lifted the Women's Rugby World Cup, as well as five Women's Six Nations Championship Grand Slams, is quite a challenge.

Simon Middleton, however, has no doubts. "I am coming into this role when women's rugby is in a great place," he said. "It is a really exciting time to be involved. For me, personally, this is a fantastic opportunity and a challenge I am really looking forward to. Being part of the team that won the World Cup last year was the pinnacle of my career but we want England Rugby to continue to have those successes."

Before taking up his dual role, Middleton had to focus on England's attempt to earn Great Britain a place at the Rio de Janeiro 2016 Olympic Games by finishing in the top four in the 2014-15 Women's Sevens World Series and the 49-year-old underlined his credentials by successfully steering the team to their goal. The Red Roses achieved their target of Olympic qualification in dramatic fashion and by the narrowest of margins, with a 15-14 defeat of the United States in a winner-takes-all final match.

"I am absolutely thrilled we have qualified Great Britain for the Olympics," Middleton said. "It has been a tough season but, round after round, we have gradually improved and in the end we got the result we needed. Of course, we didn't do it the easy way, leaving it to the dying moments of the last game and then making it go down to the wire with points difference. Looking ahead, we know we have to improve our consistency but it is certainly going to be an exciting period."

Middleton's cross-code playing career began in Union as a winger with the Knottingley club in Yorkshire. In 1991 he joined Castleford Rugby League club, where he spent six years and scored 83 tries in 170 appearances. A brief spell back in Union with Otley preceded his move to Leeds Tykes (now Carnegie) in 1998, joined the club's coaching staff at the invitation of Director of Rugby, Phil Davies in 2000.

He worked part-time until 2007, when he went full time, with particular responsibility for defence. In his 11 years at Headingley, he worked with current England men's head coach Stuart Lancaster and England Saxons and Under 20s head coach Jon Callard. Leeds were twice promoted to the Premiership and qualified for the Heineken Cup in 2003.

After leaving Leeds in 2011, Middleton stayed in Yorkshire, working with Pontefract in the North East One division. He was also backs coach for the men's county team and was Director of Rugby at Bishop Burton College. In 2014, Middleton joined the RFU, as coach of the Women's Sevens team, while his new dual contract with the RFU runs until the conclusion of the 2017 Women's Rugby World Cup.

Right: **Simon Middleton took on a dual role in February 2015, when appointed head coach of the England Women's 15-a-side team. He had been in charge of England Women's Sevens squad since 2014.**

Simon Middleton's senior coaching career

2000–11	Leeds Carnegie Academy
2014–date	England Women's Sevens head coach
2015	England Women's head coach

England Women's Under 20 Review

JUNIORS SUFFER DOUBLE DISAPPOINTMENT

The Red Roses' next generation of Test players kicked-off their season with an impressive victory over the Army but were then frustrated home and away by a powerful French side.

It was a year of change for the England Women's Under 20s with the arrival of former England captain Jo Yapp as the team's new head coach. There were also two new assistant coaches – Kevin Moggridge and Elaine Limond – while the almost total overhaul of the set-up from the previous year was highlighted when Yapp named 11 players uncapped at Under 20 level in her starting XV for the team's season opener against the Army in early February.

Perhaps inevitably a dramatically remodelled Red Roses side made a tentative start at the Aldershot Army Rugby Stadium as the home side drew first blood with an 18th-minute try. Slowly but surely the Under 20s began to find their collective feet and they levelled the scores when Worcester full-back Rachel Lund burst through the Army midfield for an eye-catching touchdown. Lichfield fly-half Sarah Nicolas converted and then added a penalty to give England a 10-5 lead at the break.

A second try for the Army after the restart temporarily pegged back England, but they rallied encouragingly and fine support play from Bristol lock Olivia Jones saw them register a second try to regain the advantage before substitute hooker Amy Cokayne added a third to seal the 25-10 success and the perfect start to the campaign.

Yapp made three changes to the team to face the French in Bordeaux later in the month. Hartpury wing Zoe Aldcroft, Bristol scrum-half Devon Holt and Lichfield prop Henrietta Burkinshaw were all promoted to the starting XV, while Lund assumed the captaincy from the injured Caity Mattinson.

England knew they would be put under severe pressure in the Stade Sainte-Germaine and although Lichfield centre Emily Wood went agonisingly close to a try in the second half before she was hauled down just metres short, the French proved too strong on home soil and ran in four tries in a 25-0 victory.

"It was a really hard fought and physical game, which we have come to expect from France," Yapp said. "We were frustrated by our performance today but, when we did play to our patterns, we did look good. The team certainly felt the pressure of the occasion, coming to France and playing in

Below: **Jo Yapp was in her first season as the new head coach of the England Women's Under 20s team.**

Right: **Emily Wood makes a clean break for England in their narrow defeat against France at Esher in March.**

"Our general performance has come a long way from the start of the season."

Jo Yapp

front of a big crowd, but we did see some good individual performances in the team. We can take plenty of things away from the match as we prepare to play them again in three weeks' time."

The head coach made significant changes to her side for the rematch. Fresh from making her senior debut for the Red Roses in the Women's Six Nations, Bristol's Sydney Gregson was named at full-back, while Holt switched from scrum-half to the wing to accommodate the return of the fit-again Mattinson. Rebecca Noon got the nod at hooker, Amy Wigley was selected in the second row and Bristol prop Abbie Parson was named captain.

The first of the season's Under 20 Anglo-French clashes ultimately had been a one-sided affair, but it was an altogether different story when the two sides renewed acquaintances at Esher in March and although England were eventually beaten again, Yapp's players this time emerged with their reputations enhanced.

The Red Roses started brightly in the opening 20 minutes and their endeavour was finally rewarded after 10 phases of play created space wide for Holt, the wing outpacing the French cover for the try. It was the only score of the first 40 minutes and England were 5-0 in front at half time.

France hit back after the restart through wing Justine Vergnaud to level proceedings and the result hung in the balance until second row Emilie Mathieu powered over for a second score for Les Bleus. England desperately went in search of the converted try to win the match but the French defence held firm and at full time the visitors were 10-5 winners.

"We are really disappointed with the loss, especially as we dominated possession in the first-half and were leading the game," Yapp admitted "Our general performance has come a long way from the start of the season and that is underlined by taking 20 points off the defeat from France last month. This was a good performance for the team but also for several individuals."

England reclaimed the
Under 20s Six Nations
from France in 2015
after beating *Les Bleus*
on the final weekend of
the tournament.

SIX NATIONS UNDER 20's (

꙰RBS

**6
NATIONS**

WINNERS 2

ENGLAND U20s IN 2015

After conquering the game's finest with their victory in the World Rugby Junior World Championship in New Zealand in June, it was back to domestic matters in 2015 as the side prepared for their Six Nations Under 20's campaign. Champions three seasons in a row, from 2011 and 2013, England had been dethroned by France in 2014 and were eager to return the championship to their collection of titles.

ENGLAND TRIUMPH

The nature of Under 20 rugby dictates that teams change significantly from season to season. As players graduate to the senior ranks the next generation are drafted in, and it was no different for England in 2015 as they parted company with most of their world champions.

There were still seven of the squad who had featured in New Zealand in the 23 for the opening game of the Six Nations Under 20's Championship against Wales, but there was also a host of new faces as England prepared for their tournament opener in Colwyn Bay.

There was also change on the touchline as England welcomed a new head coach, Jon Callard, as Nick Walshe's successor. After masterminding back-to-back Junior World Championship triumphs, Walshe had joined Gloucester's coaching staff for the 2014–15 season. Following his appointment as the RFU's new National Performance Academy Manager & International Performance Coach in September, Callard took up the Under 20s reins.

The transition however proved to be almost seamless as England recovered from an initial loss to Wales to register four consecutive wins, including a victory over the defending champions France, on the final weekend, to reclaim the Six Nations Under 20's Championship.

Under 20 Six Nations 2015

England
Rugby

ENGLAND CLAIM CHAMPIONSHIP CROWN

The eighth season of the Under 20 Six Nations Championship saw England targeting a fifth title. It was the second time in two seasons they had entered the tournament as the reigning world champions and while they had to been forced to settle for second place in the 2014 Under 20 Six Nations, behind France, 2015 proved more productive as Jon Callard marked his first campaign as head coach with the trophy.

England's first assignment as a team saw them travel to Colwyn Bay to face Wales in early February, but Callard's first assignment as coach was to select a new captain to succeed Maro Itoje. He did not look far and when he announced the squad to play Wales, it was Itoje's second row partner from the Junior World Championship final against the Springboks, Bath lock Charlie Ewels, who was handed honour of captaincy.

"Charlie is a leader," Callard explained. "He's been playing first-team rugby for Bath and has come up against France internationals Louis Picamoles, Imanol Harinordoquy and Thierry Dusautoir this season – that kind of experience is second to none and will stand us in good stead."

On becoming coach, Callard said, "I'm delighted to take on this role in what is an exciting time for English rugby. The opportunity to continue developing England talent is a real honour. The player pathway has really established itself over the last few years, and while I will be working closely with the Under 20s and the players just out of the programme, it's imperative to keep tabs on the talent coming through below that too."

England were defending an unbeaten record in the tournament against Wales, dating back to the inaugural competition in 2008, as Ewels led the team out at Parc Eirias. However, despite tries from the Harlequins duo, number 8 James Chisholm and centre Joe Marchant, the visitors could not extend the sequence and slipped to a 21-15 loss.

It was a disappointing start for the world champions, but just six days later they had the opportunity to open their account against Italy in Devonport, seizing it convincingly with a nine-try demolition of the Azzurri at Brickfields to post a 61-0 victory.

Marchant was again to the fore with a superb hat-trick, while Northampton Saints wing Howard Packman bagged a brace. Bath fly-half Rory Jennings was on target with six conversions and England were up and running.

Below: **James Chilsholm makes a break against Wales in England's narrow 21–15 defeat at Colwyn Bay.**

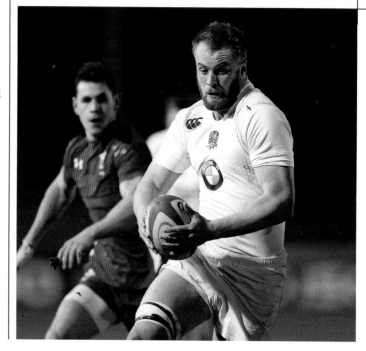

The trip to Dublin to face Ireland in round three, however, was an altogether different proposition for Callard's side. The champions in 2010, Ireland were unbeaten in their opening two games, including an impressive 37-20 win over the French, and another defeat for England would have effectively ended their title challenge.

The clash at Donnybrook was as tight as predicted. Sale scrum-half James Mitchell and Ireland fly-half Ross Byrne traded penalties during the first half, and the hosts established a slender 9-6 lead at the break.

It was crucial England scored first after the restart, and they did just that in the first three minutes. Replacement Wasps full-back Piers O'Conor made an immediate impact from the bench, latching onto a loose kick and outstripping the Irish cover to score in the corner.

The home side replied with a try from wing Stephen Fitzgerald, but as neither try was converted the margin remained three points in Ireland's favour, until Mitchell levelled proceedings with his third penalty.

The result hung in the balance, but England were indebted, for a third match in succession, to the prolific Marchant. Ten minutes from time, he stepped inside a tackle to score the try that sealed a hard-fought 19-14 win.

"This was a huge game and to come out of it with a win is massive for us," Ewels said. "Ireland came out of the blocks and had a pretty vocal home crowd behind them, but credit to our boys, we stuck at it and ground out the win.

"We knew we were in for a tough game and even when we managed to get ahead, we knew that we couldn't let up because Ireland kept pushing."

Victory sent Callard's team top of the table with two matches to play and the coach made just three changes to the team to face Scotland in Darlington, bringing in Jennings, Harlequins tighthead Seb Adeniran-Olule and Yorkshire Carnegie loosehead Paul Hill.

In 2014, the Scots had been beaten 48-15, but despite an initial three-try salvo from

> "I'm extremely proud of all of the players and the management. It's great to win and to lift the trophy and it's just reward for their efforts."
>
> **Jon Callard**

Right: **Neither the Devonport rain nor the Italian team could stop England or captain Charlie Ewels in a 61–0 victory for Jon Callard's young team.**

England, they ultimately proved sterner opposition this time around. In the first few minutes, Mitchell pounced on an overthrow at a Scottish lineout and went over for the opening try. Hill added the second when he caught Jennings' accurate cross field kick, while the third score came from Chisholm after a powerful drive from his fellow forwards. A conversion and three penalties ensured that England led 26-6 at half-time.

Scotland, however, refused to buckle and kept England scoreless after the interval, managing an unconverted try through wing Ben Robbins, but that was the only score in the second half and England ran out 26-11 winners. Although they may have been frustrated by their failure to trouble the scoreboard in the second half, the result ensured England remained in control of their own destiny and would be crowned champions with a victory over France in Brighton seven days later.

The championship decider was watched by 12,600 spectators inside the Community Stadium and they were treated to a titanic battle. They watched England subdue the champions, but only in the final quarter.

The opening 30 minutes saw Jennings and French full-back Thomas Ramos exchange successful penalties to set up the contest at 6-6. The visitors were the first to register a try, number 8 Fabien Sanconnie muscling over the line from short range after a disciplined rolling maul from the pack.

Callard's side trailed 11-6 at half-time, but the reliable boot of Jennings came to the rescue in the second half as he kicked two more penalties to make it 12-11, but there was a feeling that the home side needed to score at least one try to settle the contest.

England had to be patient, but their first five-pointer finally came in the 65th minute. Substitute scrum-half Stuart Townsend charged down a clearance kick and the prolific Marchant was quickest to react. He collected the loose ball and pirouetted in midair for his sixth try of the tournament.

Above: **Harlequins wing Joe Marchant scored a hat-trick as England Under 20s defeated Italy 61-0 at Brickfields, Devonport, on the second weekend of the championship.**

"We're half way through our season with the Junior World Cup coming up in June, and we're looking forward to heading out to Italy to defend the trophy."

Jon Callard

The conversion went wide but the lead was now 17-11.

Although France were still within striking distance, the home side delivered the decisive blow moments later. Yorkshire Carnegie hooker Jack Walker made the initial inroads into the French defence. Exeter flanker Sam Skinner provided the crucial support and his perfectly-timed offload to Sam Perkins sent the Saracens wing flying over. The excellent Jennings added the conversion to take his match total to 14 points.

France tried desperately to stage a late fightback, but England held on for a 24-11 triumph and their fourth Under 20s Six Nations title in five years.

"I'm extremely proud of all of the players and the management," Callard said. "It was a challenging game – France were extremely well drilled – but the players fronted up in the second half and ultimately deserved the win. We didn't get going in the first 40, but we kept in the game and kicked on well. It's great to win and to lift the trophy and it's just reward for their efforts.

"We're halfway through our season, with the Junior World Cup coming up in June, and we're looking forward to heading out to Italy to defend our trophy. We have a talented group of players and a huge amount of credit must go to the clubs and the Academies who put a lot of work into their guys."

Results

7 FEBRUARY 2015, PARC EIRIAS, COLWYN BAY

Wales 21   **England 15**

Tries: Belcher, Phillips   Tries: Chisholm, Marchant

Con: Jones   Con: Jennings

Pens: Jones (3)   Pen: Jennings

13 FEBRUARY, BRICKFIELDS, PLYMOUTH

England 61   Italy 0

Tries: Perkins, Owen,

Genge, Packman (2),

Marchant (3), Farnworth

Cons: Jennings (6),

Mitchell, Marchant

27 FEBRUARY, DONNYBROOK, DUBLIN

Ireland 14   **England 19**

Try: Fitzgerald   Tries: O'Conor, Marchant

Pens: Byrne (3)   Pens: Mitchell (3)

13 MARCH, NORTHERN ECHO ARENA, DARLINGTON

England 26   Scotland 11

Tries: Mitchell, Hill, Chisholm   Try: Robbins

Con: Jennings

Pens: Jennings (3)   Pens: Horne (2)

20 MARCH, COMMUNITY STADIUM, BRIGHTON

England 24   France 11

Tries: Marchant, Perkins   Try: Sanconnie

Con: Jennings

Pens: Jennings (4)   Pens: Ramos (2)

Below: **Fly-half Rory Jennings contributed 53 points to the England cause in the Six Nations Championship as the Under 20s claimed the title.**

Final Table

TEAM	P	W	D	L	F	A	PD	Tries	PTS
England	5	4	0	1	145	57	88	18	8
France	5	3	0	2	145	82	63	19	6
Scotland	5	3	0	2	115	117	-2	14	6
Wales	5	3	0	2	102	111	-9	12	6
Ireland	5	2	0	3	120	90	30	13	4
Italy	5	0	0	5	46	216	-170	6	0

IN THE SPOTLIGHT:

Jon Callard

England Rugby

Position: **National Performance Academy Manager & International Performance Coach**

Age: 49

Jon Callard has been member of the Rugby Football Union's coaching staff since joining the National Academy set-up a decade ago. He assumed a wider role in 2015 when he took charge of the England Under-20 squad ahead of their Six Nations Championship campaign.

Nurturing and developing the next generation of Test players is a significant task within any Union. Talented younger players challenging the older guard is the lifeblood of any successful international team and England have been blessed with an abundant crop of stars moving up from the Under-20 squad.

Until July 2014, head coach Nick Walshe had that job. The Under-20s' back-to-back Junior World Championship triumphs were testament to his phenomenal success, but when Walshe joined Gloucester, the RFU needed to find his replacement.

Two months later, Jon Callard was unveiled as the man to take on this role, naming the 49-year-old as their new National Performance Academy Manager & International Performance Coach, with responsibility for the both the Under-20 and Saxons sides.

"I'm delighted to take on this role in what is an exciting time for English rugby," Callard said after his appointment. "I see it as an extension of my current position and the opportunity to continue developing English talent is a real honour. The player pathway has really established itself over the last few years, and while I will be working closely with the Under-20s and the players just out of the programme, it's imperative to keep tabs on the talent coming through below that too."

Walshe was a hard act to follow, but Callard showed he was the right man for the job in 2015 as the team bounced back from losing the opening match of the Under 20 Six Nations, to win their next four and claim the title. After the Wales defeat, England beat Italy, Ireland and Scotland to set up a decider against France at the Brighton Community Stadium. The 24-11 victory secured the title and the new head coach could reflect on a successful debut campaign.

Callard won five caps for England, but played a key role in a famous victory over New Zealand at Twickenham in 1993, kicking four penalties in the 15-9 win. In his five Tests, he amassed 69 points, including 21 against Samoa in Durban in the pool stage of Rugby World Cup 1995.

He enjoyed a glittering decade of success at club level with a dominant Bath side during the 1990s. The full-back celebrated six league championship victories, including four successive title wins. But the highlight of his club career came in 1998, when he scored all of Bath's points – a try, conversion and four penalties – as they dramatically beat Brive 19-18 in the Heineken Cup final.

His journey into coaching began later in 1998, when he became assistant to Andy Robinson at Bath. Two years later he was named head coach at The Rec, before heading north in 2002 to become first team coach at Leeds. It was in his three seasons at Headingley, that the club qualified for the group stages of the Heineken Cup for the first time. Callard combined his club duties at Leeds with his role as the head coach of the England Under-21 side from 2002 to 2005. His decision to leave Leeds and join the National Academy full-time in 2005 was Carnegie's loss and the RFU's gain.

Callard's expertise with the boot persuaded then England head coach Brian Ashton to call on him to be the team's kicking coach ahead of Rugby World Cup 2007 in France.

Right: **Jon Callard steered the England Under-20s to the Six Nations title in his maiden campaign.**

Jon Callard's senior coaching career

2000–02	Bath Rugby
2002–05	Leeds Carnegie
2005–date	Rugby Football Union

Mission accomplished,
England's Sevens team
celebrate Team GB's
qualification for the Rio
2016 Olympic Games.

n Event for the Games of the XXXI Olympiad
in Rio de Janeiro in 2016

ualifi

ENGLAND SEVENS

After finishing fourth in the 2013-14 Sevens World Series, England emulated the feat in 2014-15 to ensure that Great Britain will send a Sevens team to the Olympics Games in Rio de Janeiro next year.

HSBC Sevens World Series

ENGLAND CELEBRATE BEING ON THE ROAD TO RIO

England embarked on their 2014-15 HSBC Sevens World Series campaign targeting a top four finish to secure qualification for the Rio de Janeiro 2016 Olympics Games. Simon Amor's team knew they could ill-afford any mistakes in the nine-event competition and the triumph in the Japan Sevens in April proved decisive as they sealed Great Britain's place in Brazil next year.

The return of rugby at the Olympics in 2016 – after a 92-year absence – added an extra dimension to the HSBC Sevens World Series in 2014-15, as the leading exponents of the sport's shortened format vied to be part of the Games. As the 16th edition of the tournament kicked-off in Australia in October, hopes were high England would be among the qualifiers.

The Gold Coast Sevens however began in frustrating fashion as Simon Amor's charges were beaten 21-19 by Argentina in their opening game on Day One. However, that disappointment turned to elation on Day Two when England faced defending champions New Zealand in the Cup quarter-final, and registered a stunning 31-7 victory, courtesy of a brace of tries from Phil Burgess.

Fiji denied England a place in the final but a convincing 19-0 triumph over South Africa in the third-fourth play-off match earned the squad a valuable 17 points and their bid to reach Brazil was up and running.

The Dubai and South Africa Sevens on successive weekends in December proved less rewarding for England as they lost in the Plate semi-finals on both occasions, but they returned to form with a bang at the New Zealand Sevens in February, progressing all the way to the Cup final.

Hosts New Zealand were their opponents in Wellington but, despite second-half tries from captain Tom Mitchell and John Brake – after Marcus Watson's first-half effort – England could not complete a miraculous fightback after conceding five tries to the Kiwis and they were narrowly beaten 27-21.

"It's always nice to be in a cup final," Amor said after the game. "It's why we play the game. The guys want to be competing at the highest level and winning trophies.

"We still have a long way to go with the programme, but this is a good step forward. We had a few players competing in their first tournament for us and the atmosphere in Wellington was a big factor – that experience will stand them in good stead."

A week later England were in Las Vegas for the USA Sevens and the fifth event on the Series calendar but a surprise 15-12 reverse against Canada in the pool stages on Day One set the tone for what was a

Left: **England met defending champions New Zealand seven times during the 2014–15 HSBC Sevens World Series.**

underwhelming weekend for the team. Although they registered a 26-5 win over France in the Plate semi-final, England were beaten by Australia (21-14) in the final to cast doubt on their Olympic qualification.

That doubt was only magnified following results at the prestigious Hong Kong Sevens in March. Amor's team were unbeaten in their three Pool D fixtures, but they were knocked out of the Cup by Fiji in the quarter-final, then lost to Australia again in the Plate semi-final. A modest 10-point haul from the event did nothing to bolster their hopes of that top-four finish.

"We are working hard and we're confident that will carry us through to the Olympics," insisted Mitchell. "We know what we need to work on and we've a week to do that before Tokyo. We've got a quick turnaround, but we've shown we can mix it with the best."

With three events remaining, England urgently needed a strong showing at the Japan Sevens in early April and they produced exactly that as they stormed into the final. In the showpiece game they defeated South Africa 21-14 to record their first HSBC Sevens World Series title since they winning the New Zealand Sevens in February 2013.

England beat Hong Kong (33-0) and Wales

(10-7) in their opening Pool A games in the Prince Chichibu Memorial Stadium in Tokyo and, although they lost 33-19 to Fiji in their final match on Day One, a Cup quarter-final against France awaited them.

It was a tight, low-scoring game against Les Bleus eventually settled by unconverted tries from Dan Norton and Alex Gray while two converted tries from Burgess and Charles Hayter were enough to see off Canada 14-5 in the semi-final.

The final against the Springboks was an epic tussle, but one in which England never trailed. Hayter's sixth minute score, converted by Mitchell, ensured England were level at 7-7 at half-time, and they stretched clear after the restart courtesy of tries from Watson and Burgess. Although South Africa scored the final try of the contest in the dying minutes, it was not enough to deny Amor's team a famous triumph.

"I am unbelievably proud of this team," said Mitchell. "It's a huge effort and we are so grateful to deliver this title. Our confidence is always something we are trying to build. I'm glad we stuck to our processes and really believed in what we could do. South Africa are an unbelievable team, as they have shown all series, and we were always going to have to fight to the end."

Victory and 22 points in Japan propelled England into fourth in the Sevens World Series standings and with just two events of the season to play, their destiny was back in their own hands.

The Scotland Sevens in Glasgow in May provided the penultimate weekend of action in this season's Series. Despite being held 17-17 by Australia at Scotstoun in their opening Pool A fixture, England they ensured they finished Day One unbeaten after wins over Russia and France.

Day Two brought a Cup quarter-final victory over Canada (14-7), but there was to be no successive Cup final appearance after England were edged out 5-0 by New Zealand in the last four. It was a bitter pill to swallow, but Amor's squad recovered quickly, beating the USA 24-17 in the third-fourth place play-off match to earn 17 points and, crucially, establish a 16-point cushion on the fifth-placed Wallabies ahead of the Marriott London Sevens six days later.

Below: **England's crucial triumph at the Toyko Sevens in April was the highlight of their campaign.**

Left: **England celebrate victory against New Zealand in the Cup quarter-final at the London Sevens in May**

England arrived at Twickenham knowing exactly what they had to do, and they began the weekend in style, demolishing Kenya 40-0 in their first Pool C match. The men in white knew qualification for the Rio de Janeiro 2016 Olympic Games would be confirmed with victory over Brazil in their second pool match. The tournament was also Norton's 50th HSBC World Sevens Series appearance and the prolific speedster marked the milestone occasion with two tries as England won 56-7.

The celebrations, however, had to wait as England continued their bid to win their home event. Athough they suffered a loss 22-19 to Scotland in their final pool game, England secured a Cup quarter-final meeting with New Zealand on Day Two. It was the seventh meeting between the two sides in the 2014-15 Series and after five defeats to the Kiwis, Amor's team gave home fans plenty of reasons to cheer as they scored tries from Mitchell, Watson and Warwick Lahmert to register a rousing 21-17 win.

USA were England's opponents in the last four, but there was to be no dream appearance in the final at Twickenham as the Eagles ran out 43-12 winners. And the season ended with England being edged out 26-12 by newly-crowned champions Fiji in the third-fourth place play-off game.

Those last two defeats may not have been in the script, but as the 2014-15 HSBC Sevens World Series drew to a conclusion, England could nonetheless reflect on a mission accomplished and look forward to challenging for gold in Brazil in 2016 in the guise of a combined Great Britain team.

"I am so proud of the boys," said Amor. "They have worked so hard this year and there have been some real challenges but they have kept their mental focus and managed all the expectations. We have had a few rocky bumps along the way but the work ethic from the team and leadership from Tom Mitchell has been great. This is a very special and exciting group and I am excited about what they can do in the future."

"I am unbelievably proud of this team. It is a huge effort and we are so grateful to deliver this title."

Tom Mitchell

HSBC SEVENS WORLD SERIES RESULTS

GOLD COAST SEVENS (11-12 OCTOBER 2014)

England 19	Argentina 21	(Pool D)
England 14	USA 7	(Pool D)
England 19	Canada 12	(Pool D)
England 31	New Zealand 7	(Cup QF)
England 7	Fiji 48	(Cup SF)
England 19	South Africa 0	(3/4 Playoff)

DUBAI SEVENS (5-6 DECEMBER 2014)

England 19	USA 10	(Pool C)
England 38	Kenya 0	(Pool C)
England 5	Australia 12	(Pool C)
England 7	New Zealand 29	(Cup QF)
England 19	Argentina 21	(Plate SF)

SOUTH AFRICA SEVENS (13-14 DECEMBER 2014)

England 45	Japan 0	(Pool D)
England 22	Samoa 7	(Pool D)
England 0	New Zealand 5	(Pool D)
England 7	South Africa 31	(Cup QF)
England 0	Fiji 31	(Plate SF)

NEW ZEALAND SEVENS (6-7 FEBRUARY 2015)

England 29	Papua New Guinea 0	(Pool B)
England 27	Canada 5	(Pool B)
England 5	New Zealand 24	(Pool B)
England 26	Fiji 21	(Cup QF)
England 24	Scotland 19	(Cup SF)
England 21	New Zealand 27	(Cup Final)

USA SEVENS (13-15 FEBRUARY 2015)

England 19	Argentina 17	(Pool B)
England 12	Canada 15	(Pool B)
England 21	Kenya 14	(Pool B)
England 14	South Africa 21	(Cup QF)
England 26	France 5	(Plate SF)
England 14	Australia 21	(Plate Final)

HONG KONG SEVENS (27-29 MARCH 2015)

England 26 Wales 19 (Pool D)		
England 17	Kenya 7	(Pool D)
England 21	USA 21	(Pool D)
England 12	Fiji 14	(Cup QF)
England 7	Australia 12	(Plate SF)

JAPAN SEVENS (4-5 APRIL 2015)

England 33	Hong Kong 0	(Pool A)
England 10	Wales 7	(Pool A)
England 19	Fiji 33	(Pool A)
England 10	France 0	(Cup QF)
England 14	Canada 5	(Cup SF)
England 21	South Africa 14	(Cup Final)

SCOTLAND SEVENS (9-10 May 2015)

England 17	Australia 17	(Pool A)
England 43	Russia 7	(Pool A)
England 26	France 7	(Pool A)
England 14	Canada 7	(Cup QF)
England 0	New Zealand 5	(Cup SF)
England 24	USA 19	(3/4 Playoff)

LONDON SEVENS (16-17 May 2015)

England 40	Kenya 0	(Pool C)
England 56	Brazil 7	(Pool C)
England 19	Scotland 22	(Pool C)
England 21	New Zealand 17	(Cup QF)
England 12	USA 43	(Cup SF)
England 12	Fiji 26	(3/4 Playoff)

IN THE SPOTLIGHT:

Simon Amor

A man with a wealth of experience as a player at the elite level of the shortened format of the game, Simon Amor has made the successful transition from pitch to touchline as the head coach of the England Sevens side.

England Rugby

Position: **England Sevens head coach**

Age: **36**

When Simon Amor succeeded Ben Ryan in September 2013, the England Sevens team had just finished sixth in the HSBC Sevens World Series. The new head coach knew dramatic improvement was required if England were to make it to the Rio 2016 Olympic Games.

Amor had the 2013-14 Series to start the rebuilding process before the serious business of attempting to qualify for the Games began in 2014. That 2013-14 campaign was definitely encouraging as England reached the Hong Kong Sevens final, and played in five other Cup semi-finals. When it was over, after the Marriott London Sevens in May, England's progress was shown with fourth place in the final table.

Although the team finished outside the medals at the Glasgow 2014 Commonwealth Games in July, Amor steered England to a second successive fourth-place finish and qualification for the Olympics.

There was much to admire in England's displays in 2014-15, not least two victories against defending champions New Zealand, but it was the squad's triumph in the Japan Sevens in Tokyo in April, beating South Africa in the Cup final, which highlighted the renewed collective confidence and self-belief instilled by Amor in the players. Tom Mitchell, chosen to be captain by Amor in early 2014, proved to be a fine selection, and his personal tally of 216 points in the Series were instrumental in securing a top-four finish.

Amor's success was little surprise to those who saw him represent England at Sevens. He is a man with a distinguished pedigree in the shortened form of the game. A scrum-half in the 15-man game, Amor broke into England's Sevens squad in 2001. His time on the international circuit coincided with England's golden period in the Sevens World

Series as they finished in the top three for five consecutive seasons. Under Amor's captaincy, England won the prestigious Hong Kong title four years in a row.

His finest season was in 2003-04, as England narrowly lost out to New Zealand for the overall title, but Amor's outstanding displays were recognised in December 2004, when he was named the inaugural Sevens World Series Player of the Year. In total, Amor played 43 times in the series and scored 721 points. He also won a silver medal at the Melbourne 2006 Commonwealth Games, beating Fiji in the semi-final before losing 29-21 to New Zealand.

Amor represented Cambridge University, London Irish, Blackheath, Coventry, Gloucester and Wasps at 15-a-side, and he starred for the latter two as they won the Middlesex Sevens in 2005 and 2006, respectively.

His first coaching role was with the England Women's Sevens team in 2007, and he took the team to the Rugby World Cup Sevens in Dubai two years later. England lost to eventual champions Australia in the quarter-final, but won the Plate, beating Canada 12-0 in the final.

Amor returned to club rugby in 2010, as head coach at London Scottish. The following year, Amor was promoted to the role of the Exiles' director of rugby before assuming the mantle of as England Sevens coach in 2013.

Right: **Simon Amor's second season at the helm of the England Sevens squad was a successful one.**

Simon Amor's senior coaching career

2007–08	England Women's Sevens
2010–13	London Scottish
2013–date	England Sevens

The Red Roses ensured
Great Britain will be
represented at the 2016 Rio
de Janeiro Olympic Games

Qualification Event for the Games of the XX
in Rio de Janeiro in 2016

Qualific

WOMEN'S SEVENS SERIES

The 2014-15 World Rugby Women's Sevens Series was the third edition of the tournament, but the first in which England competed as professionals following the Rugby Football Union's decision in August to award full-time contracts to 20 of England's leading female players.

The objective for Simon Middleton's squad, ahead of the opening weekend of action at the Dubai Sevens in December, was a top-four finish, a result which would secure automatic qualification for Great Britain at the 2016 Rio de Janeiro Olympic Games.

The six rounds, in Dubai, Sao Paulo, Atlanta, Langford, London and finally Amsterdam produced a roller-coaster ride of emotions, filled with unpredictabililty. It was, ultimately, a triumphant run, but qualification for Rio was not actually achieved until after the hooter had sounded to signal the completion of the final match of England's last match in the Sevens series.

Women's Sevens Series

England
Rugby

OLYMPIC JOY FOR THE RED ROSES

With six tournaments over six months in the Women's Sevens World Series ahead of them, England had precious little margin for error as they began their bid to emulate the top-four finish they achieved in 2013–14 to book Great Britain's place at the Rio 2016 Olympic Games.

When Simon Middleton unveiled his squad for the Dubai Sevens in December, the head coach had the luxury of calling on the services of five of the players who'd lifted the Women's Rugby World Cup 2014, four months earlier, and with Richmond's Abigial Chamberlain installed as captain, England began the Series in optimistic mood.

The opening day's play in The Sevens Stadium saw the Red Roses defeat Fiji (26-0), Brazil (29-7) and Canada (17-12) in Pool C to seal a place in the Cup quarter-finals the following day. However, France proved sterner opposition in the first knockout match and despite a second-half try from Jo Watmore, England lost 7-5. England rallied with Plate semi-final victory over Russia and a 19-12 success against the Fijians in the Plate Final to secure 12 points. The season was up and running.

The Brazil Sevens in Sao Paulo, in early February, produced a similar story as Middleton's charges once again claimed victory in the Plate Final, this time defeating the USA 14-5 courtesy of tries from Rachael Burford and Danielle Waterman.

"It has been a tough weekend and to be honest we deserved to finish where we did," Middleton said. "Australia were the better side in the quarter-finals, but the players responded well to that defeat and fronted up against Russia in the semi-final. We then made hard work of our final game against the USA but, in the end, we did enough. We are now fifth in the World Series and we know we have got to keep moving forward over the next four rounds to get higher up the rankings ladder."

Fifth however became sixth after the USA Sevens, in Atlanta in March, after an uncharacteristically lethargic weekend from the Red Roses, losing to Canada in the group phase and then Canada, again, and New Zealand in the knockout stages to limp home in seventh place with only eight points won.

The campaign was already at the halfway stage and England desperately needed a strong performance at the Canada Sevens, in Langford in April, to reinvigorate their challenge for Olympic qualification.

The first day brought a 19-19 draw with Fiji and a 24-14 defeat to New Zealand, the reigning champions, but the Red Roses emerged for Day Two with a steely determination and despite losing again to the Kiwis in the Cup semi-final, they held their nerve in the third-place play-off clash with France to run out 19-7 victors thanks to a try double from Natasha Brennan and another from Katy Mclean.

"We are pleased that we have made some real progress in Canada in securing our best finish of the season but we have still got a lot to work on," said Middleton's after

"There are games when you go in and you have some doubts, and there are games when you know you're going to win. Before that game, the feeling was that we were going to do this."

Abigail Chamberlain, after beating the USA in the Netherlands Sevens third-place play-off match

his team's 16-point haul. "With two legs remaining we will be working incredibly hard to ensure we do everything we can to continue to move up the series standing in our bid to secure a top four finish and Olympic qualification."

Returning to fifth place after their efforts in Canada, England looked ahead to their home event in May with renewed confidence. Initially the Red Roses faithful had plenty to cheer as their team brushed aside South Africa (28-7) and Russia (21-12) in the opening two Pool B fixtures. A 31-0 reverse against the Canadians, however, proved something of a shock to the system and for the third meeting between the two sides in succession, New Zealand were the dominant side in the Cup quarter-final on Day Two, beating Middleton's side 24-14 at the Twickenham Stoop.

England's weekend was in real danger of unravelling, but they put their earlier disappointments behind them quickly, beating Spain (10-0) in the Plate semi-final and France (10-0) in the final to secure 12 points and ensure the event was not a disaster.

The climax of the Series, the Netherlands Sevens in Amsterdam, was just five days away and England now found themselves in sixth in the standings, two points adrift of the USA in fourth and France in fifth. A grandstand finish beckoned and the Red Roses faced a weekend which would define their season.

"We have to take it one game at a time," insisted Chamberlain ahead of the all-important event. "It won't be easy as all the games are tough in this series. We know where we went wrong last weekend and hopefully we'll fix it this weekend."

Middleton's team certainly began the tournament in emphatic style, dismantling China 56-0 in their opening Pool B, match thanks to a brace of tries from Amy Wilson-Hardy. They were almost as prolific in the next game, defeating Russia 40-5 courtesy of two scores from Natasha Hunt, but Australia showed their class in the final group game, beating England 24-7 to conclude day one.

That meant the Red Roses would face New Zealand in the Cup quarter-final first up on Saturday, knowing a defeat would seriously undermine any hopes of overhauling the USA and France in the standings.

After three consecutive defeats to the Kiwis, England could have been forgiven to approaching the game with trepidation, but they showed no signs of nerves as they refused to take a backwards step. A first-minute try from Wilson-Hardy gave them a boost and although New Zealand took a 14-10 second-half lead, England secured the victory

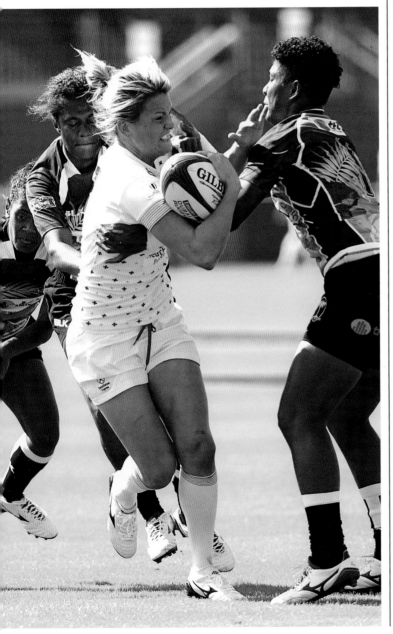

Below: **Abigail Chamberlain led the Red Roses with distinction during England's ultimately successful 2014–15 Women's Sevens Series campaign.**

they needed when Emily Scarratt went over after 12 minutes. Mclean converted and Middleton's side were 17-14 winners.

Australia once again proved England's nemesis in the Cup semi-final, winning 26-0. However, the USA's defeat to Canada in the last four, coupled with France's quarter-final loss meant the Red Roses would play the Americans in the third-place play-off match, the winner securing overall fourth place and Olympic qualification.

It was only the second meeting between the teams in the Series. England had emerged 14-5 winners in Brazil in February, but it was the USA who started stronger in the rematch, taking a 7-0 lead with a third-minute converted try from Megan Bonny. The Red Roses responded with an unconverted try from Marlie Packer so, at half time, it was 7-5 to the USA.

A try from Scarratt early in the second period gave England a precarious and precious three-point advantage, but when Jo Watmore went over in the 12th minute, England were tantalisingly close to realising their Olympic dream. The USA ensured nerves were jangling until the dying seconds with a try seconds before the hooter, but it was too little, too late and at the final whistle, the Red Roses were 15-14 winners.

The result left Middleton's team and the Eagles level on 76 points, but England were in fourth place, courtesy of a superior points difference over the course of the Series.

"It's probably been one of the best and hardest years of my life," admitted captain Abigail Chamberlain after the crucial victory over the USA at the Netherlands Sevens. "It's the dream isn't it? We've worked our backsides off to be in this position and we did it. All credit to USA because they were fighting right down to the end.

"There are games when you go in and you have some doubts, and there are games when you know you're going to win. Before that game, the feeling was that we were going to do this. We've proved that we're able to get that far, and we're only getting better."

Below: **Jo Watmore scored a crucial try against the United States at Twickenham in May in the penultimate round of the Women's Sevens World Series.**

WOMEN'S SEVENS SERIES RESULTS

DUBAI SEVENS (4–5 DECEMBER 2014)

England 26	Fiji 0	Pool C
England 29	Brazil 7	Pool C
England 17	Canada 12	Pool C
England 5	France 7	Cup QF
England 21	Russia 19	Plate SF
England 19	Fiji 12	Plate Final

CANADA SEVENS (18–19 APRIL 2015)

England 31	Spain 14	Pool A
England 19	Fiji 19	Pool A
England 12	New Zealand 24	Pool A
England 12	Canada 5	Cup QF
England 14	New Zealand 24	Cup SF
England 19	France 7	3/4 Playoff

BRAZIL SEVENS (7–8 FEBRUARY 2015)

England 31	South Africa 5	Pool C
England 17	Russia 17	Pool C
England 17	Canada 24	Pool C
England 10	Australia 29	Cup QF
England 22	Russia 12	Plate SF
England 14	USA 5	Plate Final

ENGLAND SEVENS (15–16 MAY 2015)

England 28	South Africa 7	Pool B
England 21	Russia 12	Pool B
England 0	Canada 31	Pool B
England 12	New Zealand 24	Cup QF
England 10	Spain 0	Plate SF
England 19	France 0	Plate Final

USA SEVENS (14–15 MARCH 2015)

England 33	China 7	Pool C
England 24	Brazil 0	Pool C
England 26	Canada 10	Pool C
England 0	Russia 24	Cup QF
England 12	Australia 24	Plate SF
England 31	Brazil 10	7/8 Playoff

NETHERLANDS SEVENS (22–23 MAY 2015)

England 56	China 0	Pool B
England 40	Russia 5	Pool B
England 7	Australia 24	Pool B
England 17	New Zealand 14	Cup QF
England 0	Australia 26	Cup SF
England 15	USA 14	3/4 Playoff

Right: **Despite the best efforts of Bui Baravilala, Emily Scarrett dives over in the corner for the vital try in the 3rd Place Play-Off match against the United States in the Netherlands Sevens.**

Rio 2016 Olympic Games

England
Rugby

RUGBY SEVENS SET FOR BRAZILIAN CARNIVAL

In late summer 2016, Rugby will have the opportunity to showcase itself in a front of an estimated global audience of more than four billion. The shortened format of the sport – Rugby Sevens – will feature at the Rio 2016 Olympic Games, 92 years after it last graced the world's greatest multi-sport festival.

The last time rugby appeared on the Olympic schedule was the Paris 1924 Games, and just three nations participated in the 15-a-side tournament. The entrants were hosts France, the United States of America and Romania, and only three matches were played. The USA defied the odds and won a second straight gold medal, defeating France 17-3 in the final, having won the event at the Antwerp 1920 Olympic Games.

Paris 1924 was the fourth Olympic Games Rugby tournament, the first two having been at the Paris 1900 and London 1908 Games. The USA's triumph proved to be the end of the line as an Olympic sport for almost a century.

Its initial introduction in 1900 had come at the insistence of International Olympic Committee founder Baron Pierre de Coubertin, a devotee to the game after his visits to Rugby School in the late nineteenth century. De Coubertin stood down as President of the IOC in 1925 and his successor, Henri de la Baillet-Latour, proved less of an admirer of the sport and rugby disappeared from the schedule.

In Rio de Janeiro next year, however, Rugby finally returns to the Olympic Games, albeit in the abbreviated Sevens format. And, thanks to the collective efforts of both the men's and women's teams, Great Britain will

Left: **The United States are the reigning Olympic Rugby champions after their surprise victory over hosts France at the 1924 Games in Paris.**

be represented in both tournaments.

It was agreed by the RFU and the Welsh and Scottish Unions, that England would be the nominated nation in terms of qualification for the men and women and, courtesy of top-four finishes for the teams, coached by Simon Amor and Simon Middleton, respectively in the World Rugby Sevens Series campaigns in 2014-15, Team GB can now start planning for Rio.

Both tournaments in Brazil will feature 12 countries and although the exact make-up of both British squads are yet to be finalised, the chance to compete for a coveted gold medal is now a reality.

The champions will be decided over two days of play in August in the Deodoro Stadium, on the outskirts of Rio, a purpose built 20,000-capacity venue which will also stage the Games' riding events and parts of the modern pentathlon.

As hosts Brazil, qualified automatically for both tournaments and, following the 2014-15 Sevens World Series, they will be joined in the men's competition by Fiji, South Africa, New Zealand and Great Britain. In the women's tournament, New Zealand, Canada and Australia sealed their places at the Games alongside Team GB. The remaining qualifiers will be determined by regional play-offs and a world recharge tournament.

The 2012 London Olympic Games had a worldwide television audience estimated at 3.6 billion in 220 territories. The global audience for the Rio Games next year is expected to surpass four billion and England head coach Stuart Lancaster is in no doubt that such levels of exposure represent a priceless chance for the game to promote itself.

"It's an opportunity to take the sport of rugby way beyond the current rugby playing nations," he said. "I think it will be very popular as a spectacle, and we know how seriously the southern hemisphere teams will take it. We already know New Zealand are aiming to peak not just at the Rugby World Cup 2015, but also at the Olympics in 2016, so Team GB must be ready to compete against them.

"I think it will be even bigger for the women's game. The sevens environment in Rio is going to be unbelievable for the women and the sport in general, so we need to make sure we've got a truly competitive team out there – well coached, well managed and well prepared."

Great Britain's Olympic rugby record is odd: the team has never won a match but has won two silver medals. The 1900 Paris Games saw the Moseley Wanderers club representing Great Britain and they were beaten 27-8 by France. The French also won the final, against Germany, but both Germany and Great Britain won silver medals.

The Cornwall county team played as Great Britain at the London 1908 Olympic Games, but they lost 32–3 to Australasia at the White City Stadium. This time, there were only two teams in the competition, so Great Britain "won" another silver medal.

Below: **After almost a century, Rugby will return to the Olympics when Rio de Janeiro host the 2016 Games.**

England Saxons were too strong for the Wolfhounds in their clash at Musgrave Park.

ENGLAND SAXONS

It was a quiet 2015 for England's second string side with only one fixture – a heavyweight encounter away to the Ireland Wolfhounds – but Jon Callard's side seized their opportunity to press collective and individual claims for a senior call-up with a determined display in Cork.

England Saxons

England Rugby

SLADE STARS AS THE WOLFHOUNDS ARE DEFEATED

In their only engagement of the year, the Saxons headed to Cork in late January to tackle the Ireland Wolfhounds and erase memories of the side's 14-8 home defeat to the same opposition 12 months earlier.

When head coach Jon Callard unveiled his Saxons starting XV to face Ireland at Musgrave Park, it was an announcement dominated by one high-profile selection. Included in the team was rugby league convert Sam Burgess, a mere two months after he had made his union debut for Bath in the Aviva Premiership.

The 26-year-old's call-up, at inside centre to partner Wasps' Elliot Daly in England's midfield, was undoubtedly headline news but the former Bradford Bulls and England star – who had played for 78 minutes in Australian 2014 RL's grand final with a broken cheekbone and still won the man of the match award – joined one of the most powerful Saxons line-ups in recent memory.

In total, Callard named nine full internationals to start in Cork. Northampton scrum-half Lee Dickson, capped 18 times, was handed the captaincy while Saracens' Chris Ashton and Harlequins' Marland Yarde were selected on the respective wings. The front row was an all-Test combination of Matt Mullan, Rob Webber and Henry Thomas, with flanker Matt Kvesic, number eight Thomas Waldrom and full-back Chris Pennell completing the contingent of senior England players.

"The game against the Wolfhounds will be a difficult and tough match for us," Callard conceded before kick-off. "But the group is excited about it and the opportunity to put on an England shirt. The team is one of the strongest Saxons sides selected and every player knows the importance of this match with potential of claiming a spot in the senior squad for the RBS 6 Nations campaign and the World Cup later in year."

The opening quarter of the contest was attritional rather than expansive, and it was not until the 22nd minute that England were able to make a significant impression on the Irish defence.

The breakthrough eventually came courtesy of good driving work from Webber

"Stuart Lancaster talked to the squad on Monday and told the players he expected them to win and ... to be hurting that they've been left out of the senior squad."

Jon Callard

Ireland 9
England 18

Date: **30 January 2015**
Stadium: **Musgrave Park, Cork**
Attendance: **8,200**
Referee: **Neil Hennessy (Wales)**

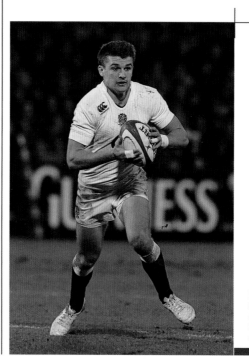

Left: **Exeter's Henry Slade enhanced his chances of a senior England call-up with a superb display in Cork.**

and lock Matt Garvey. Waldrom and second row Dave Ewers continued the momentum with a fine interchange and when the ball went wide, Daly was on hand to continue the attack. He was hauled down five metres short but with the defence in full retreat, fly-half Henry Slade identified the gap around the fringes of the ruck and sliced through for the opening try.

The young Exeter playmaker was off target with the conversion but he made no mistake with a penalty attempt, three minutes later, and England had led 8-0. Slade and his Irish opposite number Ian Madigan then exchanged penalties so the the visitors enjoyed an 11-3 half-time lead.

Featuring 13 internationals in their ranks, the Wolfhounds came out for the second half in predictably determined fashion. After Madigan had kicked his second and third penalties, on 49 and 57 minutes, respectively, England's lead was down to a slender two points and the result was in the balance.

There was to be no more scoring until the penultimate minute of the match, and it went to the Saxons to seal the victory. The pack secured lineout possession deep in Irish territory. A drive took them closer to the line and when the ball was released, first try scorer Slade turned provider as he found Christian Wade – who had replaced Yarde – close to the touchline and he sidestepped one tackler and evaded a second to touch down. Slade added the extras for a personal haul of 13 points in the 18-9 triumph.

"Stuart Lancaster talked to the squad on Monday and told the players he expected them to win and expected them to be hurting that they've been left out of the senior squad," Callard said after the final whistle. "I'm very proud of our attacking rugby. The players gave everything against a good Irish side. We scored two tries and nilled them on tries, which was very impressive. The players deserve all the credit."

Irish Wolfhounds 9		England Saxons 18	
15	Felix JONES (c)	15	Chris PENNELL
14 →	Fergus McFADDEN	14	Chris ASHTON
13	Keith EARLES	13	Elliot DALY
12	Gordon D'ARCY	12 →	Sam BURGESS
11 →	Craig GILROY	11 →	Marland YARDE
10	Ian MADIGAN	10	Henry SLADE
9 →	Kieran MARMION	9 →	Lee DICKSON (c)
1 →	Jack McGRATH	1 →	Matt MULLEN
2 →	Richardt STRAUSS	2 →	Rob WEBBER
3 →	Mike ROSS	3	Henry THOMAS
4	Iain HENDERSON	4 →	Matt GARVEY
5 →	Mike McCARTHY	5 →	James GASKELL
6	Dominic RYAN	6	Dave EWERS
7 →	Sean O'BRIEN	7	Matt KVESIC
8	Jack CONAN	8	Thomas WALDROM

REPLACEMENTS		REPLACEMENTS	
2 ←	16 Rob HERRING	2 ←	16 Luke COWAN DICKIE
1 ←	17 Michael BENT	1 ←	17 Alex WALLER
3 ←	18 Nathan WHITE		18 Jake COOPER-WOOLLEY
5 ←	19 Robbie DIACK	4 ←	19 Maro ITOJE
7 ←	20 Eion McKEON	5 ←	20 Carl FEARNS
9 ←	21 Isaac BOSS	9 ←	21 Joe SIMPSON
11 ←	22 Noel REID	11 ←	22 Ollie DEVOTO
14 ←	23 Andrew CONWAY	12 ←	23 Christian WADE

SCORES

SCORES

Tries: Slade (22), Wade (79)

Con: Slade (80)

Pens: Madigan (39, 49, 57)

Pens: Slade (25, 40)

Right: Wasps' Christian Wade came off the bench to score a late second try for the Saxons in Ireland.

IN PROFILE:

Henry Slade

Mercurial Henry Slade enjoyed a superb breakthrough campaign in 2014-15 and after a star turn for the England Saxons against the Wolfhounds, he looks destined to enjoy a long and prolific Test career.

England Rugby

Position: **Fly-half/ Centre**

Age: **22**

Height: **1.88 m**

Weight: **85.7 kg**

Under 20s Caps: **13**

Saxons Caps: **3**

When Stuart Lancaster unveiled his 50-man Rugby World Cup 2015 training squad in May, it was testament to Slade's meteoric rise that no-one was surprised to see his name on the head coach's list.

Whether he makes the cut in Lancaster's final 31-man squad remains to be seen but, after a series of dazzling displays for the Chiefs in the Aviva Premiership in 2014-15, there seems little doubt that, in Slade, England have a genuine star in the making.

"It's nice to have that knowledge that I'll be there and have a chance to stake my claim," he said after his call-up. "Everyone likes to feel they're ready for that next step. I feel I'm capable, but it's not up to me. It doesn't get any bigger than a home Rugby World Cup and of course I'd love to be involved. Who wouldn't? But I realise I'm still some way down the pecking order and have plenty to do."

Slade first registered on the England radar during the World Rugby Junior World Championship in France in 2013, pulling the strings majestically for Nick Walshe's Under 20 side at fly-half. He scored 13 points in the final as England beat Wales 23-15 to be crowned world champions for the first time.

He had made his first team Premiership debut for the Chiefs earlier in 2013, but it was in 2014-15 that he established himself as one of the first names on Rob Baxter's team sheet, Slade started all 22 Premiership games and scored 150 points as Exeter narrowly missed out on reaching the end-of-season play-offs.

His outstanding club form was rewarded with by a place in Jon Callard's Saxons team to face the Ireland Wolfhounds in Cork in January 2015. He had made two appearances as replacement for England's second string in 2014, against the Wolfhounds and Scotland 'A', but this time Slade made the starting XV. He

responded with a reassuringly mature display at Musgrave Park, scoring a try, conversion and two penalties in England's 18-9 victory.

The performance in Ireland did not go unnoticed by Lancaster and, in March, he was drafted into the senior squad as injury cover ahead of the match with Scotland, but he was not in the matchday 23.

The only serious question mark that still hangs over him is his best position. Lancaster called Slade up as a possible replacement for centre Brad Barritt, but he made his reputation with the Under 20s at fly-half and, in 2014-15, the Chiefs played him at 10, 12 and 13.

Slade's path to the England number 10 shirt is currently blocked by the considerable talents of George Ford and Owen Farrell, but he can take inspiration from former Under 20 team-mates Anthony Watson and Jack Nowell, both of whom have graduated from the class of 2013 into Lancaster's senior side.

"I have always been a 10 before, but played a little bit of centre, but never 13 before this season," he said. "For the last pre-season match, when the team was emailed through, and I was at 13, I thought it was a typo but I've enjoyed it there. That pre-season game went all right and from there each game I was learning and now I feel pretty comfortable."

Success and potential full Test recognition however has not come without significant challenges and, since 2011, Slade has had to live with Type 1 diabetes and the obstacles managing his condition has presented.

"Getting the diagnosis at 18 was pretty tough to take," he admitted. "My dad had it as well so I knew how it would affect my life and how organised I was going to have to be. Still, while the other lads get their supplements and beetroot shakes before a match, I get a nice big cup of jelly babies, so it's not all bad."

Right: Henry Slade emerged as one of the most exciting talents in the English game during the 2014–15 season.

England Counties Rugby

DOUBLE TRIUMPH FOR COUNTIES TEAM

Tasked with a home game against Scotland in late February and a trip across the Channel to tackle France the following month, the England Counties team faced a testing fixture list in 2015 but emerged after 160 minutes of endeavour without conceding a try and two significant victories under their belt.

Represented by players at clubs outside the top two – full-time professional – tiers of the domestic game, the England Counties began the year hoping to expunge memories of defeats to Ireland and France the previous season, and kicked-off their campaign with a first-ever meeting with the Scotland Club XV at Fylde's Woodlands Memorial Ground.

Old Albanians and Hertfordshire flanker Billy Johnson was named captain of a squad containing seven uncapped players for the ground-breaking fixture and with assistant coach Steve Shanahan of Plymouth Albion temporarily in charge in the absence of head coach Steve Pope, who was away on compassionate leave, England were ready for the fray.

The opposition may have been unfamiliar, but England soon had the measure of their visitors and, once Sandal scrum-half Joe

Bedford had darted over for the game's opening try, England were never in danger of defeat.

A five-metre scrum provided the platform for England's second score, to the delight of the crowd as home flanker Evan Stewart barged over and although the Counties had to wait for the second-half to pierce the Scottish defence again, four more tries followed.

Skipper Johnson restored momentum after the restart, while Blackheath loosehead prop Aston Croall galloped over in the corner after a quick tap penalty by Bedford for the fourth try.

Another tap and go by the home side put Ealing Trailfinders fly-half James Love over for the fifth from the bench but the final and perhaps biggest cheer of the afternoon was reserved for substitute scrum-half Jordan Dorrington, the Fylde No.9 going over from

Below: **England Counties were unbeaten in 2015 after registering impressive victories over Scotland and France.**

Above: **Victory over the Scotland Club XV in Fylde was the perfect start to the campaign for Steve Pope's squad.**

short range to wrap up a comprehensive 37-3 victory on his home ground.

"I thought they were outstanding," Shanahan said after the final whistle. "The most pleasing thing was their defence. Not to concede a try in a Test match is a credit to them and their character, the intensity and the work rate they showed.

"It's the opportunity to put an England shirt on, which they are never likely to do at the top, top level. It's the chance to work in a full-time environment with professional coaches, and the chance to play with players they face every week in and week out in the National Leagues."

Three weeks later England were in Perigueux to play the France Federal XV and having narrowly gone down 16-15 to the same

opponents 12 months earlier, Counties were under no illusions the scale of the challenge that lay ahead.

Johnson was again named as captain, and Pope was back in place as head coach, but heavy rain inside the Stade Francais Rongieras meant a repeat of England's six-try salvo against the Scots was never going to happen. The match became something of a war of attrition and a battle of nerves between the respective kickers.

Fortunately for England, they had Fylde's fly-half Chris Johnson in the ranks, and he was accuracy personified, successfully kicking all of his eight penalty chances. Johnson kicked the first four penalties of the match, but the French responded with four of their own to level it at 12-12. But England kept their discipline better and after another four Johnson kicks, at full-time it was a relieved and wet Counties side which had won 24-15.

"It was a bit of an arm-wrestle, but the boys really ground it out," said Pope. "There were lots of mistakes and it was a bit of cauldron atmosphere, but the boys stayed very composed. We took the points when we got the opportunity and Chris [Johnson] put them away.

"To play two spring internationals and not concede a try is something that we are very pleased with. We think this is the first time we have won both spring internationals and it's the first time we have won in France for a long time. We are absolutely delighted. For the boys to come together in such a short space of time typifies what the Counties is all about.

"I'm particularly pleased for James [Shanahan] as assistant coach because he stepped up when I couldn't travel up to Fylde for the Scotland game. He made such a big impact that there and held things together. I enjoy working with him and things really seem to flow."

"Not to concede a try in a Test match is a credit to them and their character, the intensity and the work rate they showed."

Steve Shanahan

England Students Rugby

England Rugby

PORTUGAL AND WALES ARE BEATEN

A busy year saw the England Students tackle a Portugal XV before facing their French and Welsh counterparts and, after registering two victories in three internationals, it was a campaign on which head coach Aaron James could reflect with significant satisfaction.

When James unveiled his matchday squad of 23 for the season-opener against Portugal in Lisbon in January, it was a group of players brimming with talent and potential, but short of experience. Just seven of the squad had represented England Students previously and although Bath University number eight Freddie Clarke returned to the fold as captain of the side, after making his debut in 2014, the team was nonetheless something of an unknown quantity.

Their performance in Lisbon however betrayed few signs of nerves as all 17 of England's new boys made their Students bow in a convincing 32-16 win featuring four tries from the visitors. The early exchanges saw the two sides trade two penalties apiece, but it was England who made the decisive move, minutes before half-time, when Hartpury full back Alex Brown touched down for the first try to establish a 13-6 advantage at the break.

England did not relinquish their lead throughout the second period, and further tries from Exeter University scrum-half Rob Coote, UCL flanker Seb Nagle-Taylor and St Mary's wing Jack Rossiter ensured England began their year on a high.

"The squad worked hard all week for this win and I'm pleased they got the result," said James. "All 23 played for a decent amount of time, which is traditionally what we try to do in Portugal, and the performance didn't suffer from bringing our replacements on, proving our strength throughout the squad."

There were 10 changes to the squad to face the France Universities in April in what is traditionally the Students' most testing fixture of their season and, despite a resilient display in the Stade Paul Chandon in Eperney, they could not claim a rare success against Les Bleus.

Trailing 13-0 in the first half, the highlight of the contest, from an England perspective, came when Hartpury centre George Boulton burst through the French defence after a phase of sustained pressure for a try. Leeds Beckett fly-half Will Cargill knocked over the conversion to reduce the arrears to 13-7 but it was as close as England could get to their hosts. When the final whistle sounded, France had run out 28-7 winners.

"We were unable to maintain pressure for any period of time," conceded assistant coach Ian Davies. "The French did not do anything fancy but our errors and general lack of accuracy enabled them to have control for large periods of the game."

England had almost a month to reflect on their disappointment across the Channel before facing Wales at the Caerphilly Centre of Sporting Excellence in early May and as the fixture approached, James opted to make a raft of changes to his starting XV. Nine players who had started against the French dropped out of the side, and skipper Clarke switched from No. 8 to the second row. Amongst those called up were Exeter University scrum-half Sam Waltier for his Students debut, in place of Nagle-Taylor, while a revamped front row saw Leeds Beckett prop Sam Rodman and Oxford hooker Nick Gardner included at the expense of Hartpury's Mike Flook and Exeter's Paul Davis, respectively.

"The squad worked hard all week for this win and I'm pleased they got the result."

Aaron James

The game was a roller-coaster affair, in which the home side repeatedly forced England errors, but James's side stood firm during the inevitable periods of Welsh dominance. Tries from Clarke, Waltier, Loughborough replacement fly-half Josh Sharp and Leeds Beckett centre Lewis Jones ensured England were celebrating after the final whistle after an entertaining 29-26 victory.

Below: **England Students concluded their season with a narrow 29-26 victory over Wales Students in Caerphilly.**

"I thought the performance of Sam Waltier on debut was particularly pleasing," said Davies after a game in which seven other players won their first Students cap. "He kept the team moving forward throughout the match. Although he has played well throughout the campaign, I also thought Freddie Clarke really stamped his authority on the match and demonstrated why he has secured a contract in the Championship for next season."

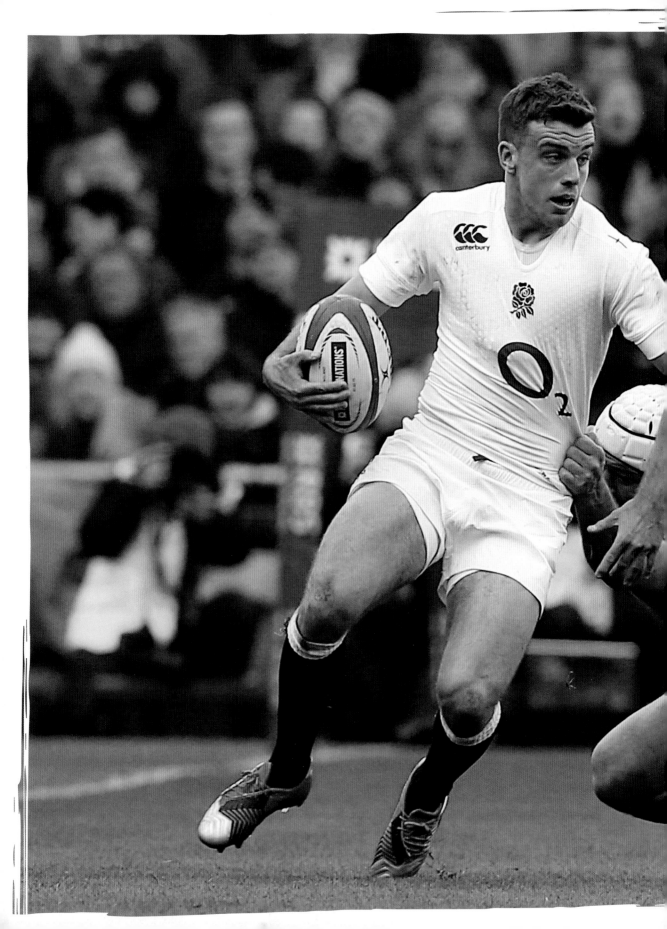

THE PLAYERS

England's men and women delivered a series of hugely entertaining displays in 2015 in their respective Six Nations Championship campaigns, and there were some spectacular individual performances from players in all the teams.

PLAYERS TO WATCH:
ENGLAND MEN

Competition for Test places in a Rugby World Cup year is always particularly intense and so it proved in early 2015 as England players focused on growth during the RBS 6 Nations and one final chance to impress head coach Stuart Lancaster on the international stage before England began their bid to lift the Webb Ellis cup in September and October.

The ferocious battle for a place in the starting XV was the catalyst for some stunning displays in the Aviva Premiership and from the front row through to full-back, Lancaster's team were in outstanding form despite being denied the title by the narrowest of margins.

From an English perspective, the focus during the tournament was on youth, as many of the more recent additions to the squad made the biggest impact, signalling the arrival of a bright new generation of England stars.

Left: Stuart Lancaster's young England team produced some stunning attacking displays during the 2016 RBS 6 Nations Championship.

England
Rugby

IN PROFILE:

George Ford

The top points scorer in this year's RBS 6 Nations Championship, Bath fly-half George Ford brought dynamism to England's attacking play throughout the tournament.

Position: **Fly-half**
Age: **22**
Height: **1.75m**
Weight: **84kg**
Caps: **11**
Points: **109 (2T, 18C, 20PG, 1DG)**

There's an old saying that if you're good enough, you're old enough. Many young players have proved the point at Test level and, in 2015, it was Ford's turn to stylishly demonstrate that age is no barrier to making an impact on the international stage.

He was aged just 21 when the competition began in early February – he celebrated his 22nd birthday two days after victory against Scotland in the Calcutta Cup the following month. With just six England caps – and only two starts – the prospect of pulling the strings at number 10 for Stuart Lancaster's side must have been a daunting one.

Some players might have withered in such a spotlight, but Ford clearly relished the pressure and responsibility and his natural attacking instincts with the ball in hand gave England a cutting edge which yielded a flood of tries during the tournament.

It was certainly no coincidence that with Ford calling the shots, England scored 18 tries in the Championship, equalling their haul in 2003 when the team last claimed the Grand Slam. Ford himself touched down twice – against Scotland and France, both at Twickenham – and he also delivered seven scoring passes for team-mates. No other player in the RBS 6 Nations Championship was more creative in terms of assists.

His haul of 75 points in five matches – the 25 in the finale against the French took him past the 100-point mark in Tests – was also the highest in the championship, eclipsing vastly more experienced players, such as Wales full-back Leigh Halfpenny and Ireland fly-half Jonathan Sexton.

Ford's international career remains very much in its infancy but the case he made in the RBS 6 Nations in 2015 to retain the number 10 jersey going into the Rugby World Cup and beyond was as convincing as it was cultured.

IN PROFILE:

Joe Marler

Appearing in his third RBS 6 Nations Championship, Harlequins prop Joe Marler came of age, with some irresistible scrummaging displays and a series of energetic performances in open play.

Position: **Prop**
Age: **24**
Height: **1.84m**
Weight: **110kg**
Caps: **31**
Points: **0**

The role of the modern prop is almost unrecognisable from that of their predecessors. Today's front-rowers must still stand firm in the battle up front, but they are now as critically appraised for their contribution around the pitch as they are at the scrum.

By both criteria Joe Marler enjoyed a fine 2015 RBS 6 Nations Championship. It was the first time the Harlequins captain – he was appointed for the 2014–15 season to allow Chris Robshaw, the national skipper, to concentrate on those duties – started all five games and he rewarded Stuart Lancaster's faith in him with an impact on the tournament which could simply not be overlooked.

In the tight Marler was immense. England lost just two scrums on their own feed throughout the whole tournament and, alongside Dan Cole and Dylan Hartley, the loose-head gave England a rock-solid platform in the set-piece. Conversely, Lancaster's first choice front row stole opposition scrum ball nine times thanks to Marler and Co's muscular efforts.

Marler, first capped against South Africa in Durban in 2012 and an ever present in the three-Test series against the All Blacks last summer, was equally impressive in broken play. He made 13 carries during the tournament, but it was his robust defensive work which caught the eye as England came so close to claiming the title.

In total, Marler made 46 tackles in the RBS 6 Nations. None of his front row colleagues made more in the victories over Scotland (eight) or France (13), and no player in England's front five delivered more stops (11) than him in the win over Italy.

Competition for places in England's front row remains fierce ahead of the Rugby World Cup but, ahead of the tournament, Marler could not have done more to stake his claim as England's premier loosehead.

England
Rugby

IN PROFILE:

Ben Youngs

Competition for the coveted England No 9 shirt has rarely been fiercer, but a series of scintillating displays from the Leicester Tiger Ben Youngs during the 2015 RBS 6 Nations underlined his status as one of Stuart Lancaster's first choice scrum-halves.

Position: **Scrum-half**

Age: **25**

Height: **1.78m**

Weight: **92kg**

Caps: **47**

Points: **45 (9T)**

When Youngs first broke into the England Test side in 2010, debuting from the bench against Australia in Perth, Harlequins' Danny Care was the player charged with pulling the strings for the men in white.

The rivalry between these two has raged ever since, with Northampton's Lee Dickson and Saracens' Richard Wigglesworth also pushing hard for inclusion. England thus are blessed with four outstanding scrum-halves.

In the 2014 RBS 6 Nations it was Care in pole position, but Youngs returned to the fray and Lancaster's starting line-up for the opening game of 2015 against Wales in Cardiff and the 25-year-old seized the opportunity with real conviction.

Youngs was magnificent throughout the tournament, collecting the Man of the Match award twice – after the victories over Scotland and France – while his three tries in the Championship showcased his full array of attributes.

His try against Italy at Twickenham – his first for England in almost three years – was all about his predatory instincts. In the 55th minute, he took a quick tap-penalty to catch the Azzurri completely flatfooted and he jinked his way between the uprights from short range.

The first of his two tries against the French was a lesson in support play. A break from Jonathan Joseph, followed by good hands from Mike Brown and George Ford, saw England make deep inroads into the Italina defence, and Youngs was on hand to take the scoring the pass, neatly pirouetting through a tackle for the score.

His second try displayed his physical power as Brown again turned the French defence. From the resulting ruck, Youngs broke away and burst through flanker Bernard le Roux's

attempted tackle to touch down.

With his three rivals desperate to dislodge him, Youngs is unlikely to become complacent but his form in early 2015 illustrated he had returned to the top of his

England Rugby

IN PROFILE:

Jack Nowell

Less than two years after starring for England in their Junior World Championship triumph in France, Nowell was in devastating form in his second RBS 6 Nations campaign.

Position: **Wing**
Age: **22**
Height: **1.81m**
Weight: **87kg**
Caps: **8**
Points: **20 (4T)**

The enviable conveyor belt of talent being produced by the England Under-20 set-up is one which bodes well for the future of Stuart Lancaster's senior side. Although some of the young players may have to wait a little bit longer for their chance to shine in the bright lights at full Test level, Exeter Chiefs wing Jack Nowell is one who has already made a supremely successful transition.

He was first capped against France in Paris in the 2014 RBS Six Nations, but then underwent knee surgery later in the season. It forced Nowell to miss not only England's summer tour of New Zealand and also the QBE Autumn Internationals, but he was back on the Test scene in 2015, and he seemed to be better than ever.

Nowell replaced Gloucester's Jonny May in the starting XV for the final three fixtures of the RBS 6 Nations Championship and his impact in those matches was spectacular. He crossed for three tries – joint-second in the Championship and also went on to lead all players in terms of metres made, clean breaks and defenders beaten.

His first try came against Scotland at Twickenham, deft footwork taking him over in the corner, and he added two more scores to his burgeoning Test CV with a brace against France, also at HQ, his second try a perfect illustration of his intelligence and pace as he picked an irresistible line through the heart of Les Bleus' midfield.

Those tries however were only half the story. In those three RBS Six Nations matches, Nowell ran for 326 metres, made nine clean breaks and left 16 defenders trailing in his wake.

His Test career still may be a work in progress, but he has convincingly demonstrated, in just eight matches, that he has the raw ingredients to score many more international tries.

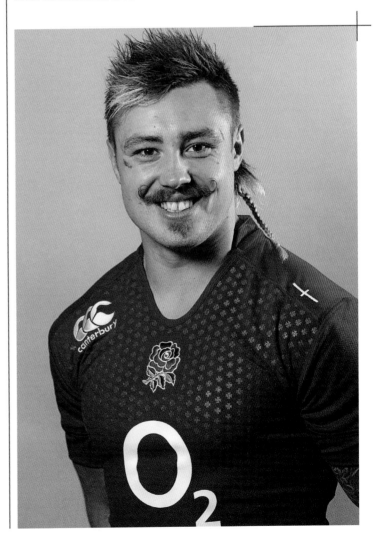

PLAYERS TO WATCH:
ENGLAND WOMEN

Ambitious international teams can ill afford to stagnate, and England were certainly mindful of the lesson in 2015 as interim head coach Nicola Ponsford drafted in eight uncapped players into the Red Roses squad during the course of the Women's Six Nations Championship.

In many ways, Ponsford's hand was forced as England had to deal with the international retirement of many of the team's Rugby World Cup winners, and the absence of others playing on the Women's Sevens World Series circuit, but the losses paved the way for a new generation of players to lay down their markers at Test level.

Many of those presented with the opportunity did exactly that and, although the Red Roses were unable to add the Six Nations Championship title to their Rugby World Cup crown, the season underlined that England possess a rich seam of new talent for the future.

Left: The Women's
Six Nations
Championship
proved a transitional
tournament for the
England squad.

IN PROFILE:

Tamara Taylor

A member of the starting XV who were crowned world champions in Paris in 2014, Tamara Taylor was in sparkling form once again for the Red Roses in 2015.

Position: **Lock**
Age: **33**
Height: **1.80m**
Weight: **83kg**
Caps: **83**

If Darlington Mowden Park's stalwart lock had decided to hang up her boots after England's victory over Canada in the final of Women's Rugby World Cup 2014, it would have been a triumphant conclusion to a glittering international career.

The Women's Rugby World Cup 2014 final was her 76th Test appearance for England and, after featuring in the 2006 and 2010 Rugby World Cups and almost a decade of loyal service for the Red Roses, no-one could have begrudged Taylor's decision to retire on a high. However, the 33-year-old resolved to play on and her displays in the Women's Six Nations 2015 were proof that, like a fine wine, she continues to improve with age.

Taylor began the Championship as England's captain, deputising for Katy Mclean who was on Sevens duty in Brazil, and although she relinquished the role after the fixtures against Wales and Italy, Taylor's influence on the side was undiminished.

Her leadership was magnificent as England despatched Italy 39-7 at the Stoop in February, the team's first win in 2015, but her most dynamic performance arguably came the following month when Scotland visited Darlington's Northern Echo Arena.

It was Taylor's 80th cap – on her home ground – and she marked the occasion with a barnstorming all-round display in which she scored one of England's eight tries, appearing on Mclean's shoulder in the sixth minute to take the pass and power through two Scottish tacklers. Taylor's dynamic contributions throughout the match caught the eye, most notably featuring twice in the loose in the build-up to a try for full-back Fiona Pocock.

There will, inevitably, come the day when Taylor does decide to end her long stint in the engine room of the England pack but, on the evidence of her performances during this year's Women's Six Nations Championship, provided she stays fit and is enjoying her rugby, it will not be anytime soon.

England Rugby

IN PROFILE:

Ceri Large

Ceri Large was an ever-present for the Red Roses during the Women's Six Nations Championship in 2015, stylishly carving out a new role for herself in the England midfield.

Position: **Fly-half/**
Centre
Age: **24**
Height: **1.73m**
Weight: **74kg**
Caps: **37**

The story of Worcester fly-half's international career has been one dominated by her rivalry with Katy Mclean for the coveted number 10 shirt. They have vied for the fly-half berth ever since Large made her Test debut against France in 2011 and when both have been fit, they have presented England with a welcome selection dilemma.

Large was the Red Roses' number 10 throughout the Women's Six Nations in 2013, but Mclean returned to the playmaker role in the 2014 Championship last year. Then, while Large was named at fly-half for the group games in Rugby World Cup 2014, Mclean started in the semi-final and final.

This year, however, England interim head coach Nicola Ponsford was determined to harness both talents in the side and for four of the five Six Nations matches, Large started at inside centre while Mclean remained at fly-half. She was a revelation in her new position, bringing mdifield creativity to an England team which had failed to score a point in the tournament-opening loss to Wales. Following Large's switch to the three-quarters, England registered six tries in the victory over Italy at the Twickenham Stoop and eight more against Scotland in Darlington.

Large's personal highlight in the competition came against the Scots in March when she dived over from short range for the Red Roses' third try, but it was her distribution, vision and stubborn defence over the course of the whole championship which confirmed her as a centre of genuine international class. Her

partnership with Abigail Brown has got better with each successive Test and, still aged only 24, Large has many more years of Test rugby, whether it be a fly-half or centre, ahead of her.

England
Rugby

IN PROFILE:

Hannah Gallagher

A standout performer in the back row of the England pack, 2015 was the year in which Hannah Gallagher emerged from the shadow of another Red Roses legend to become one in her own right.

Position: **Flanker**
Age: **23**
Height: **1.70m**
Weight: **74kg**
Caps: **25**

When England lifted the Rugby World Cup in Paris in August, the joy was tinged with sadness. The initial elation was of course overwhelming but the following month the inevitable news came that some of the longer-serving members of the squad would take their leave of Test rugby.

Flanker Maggie Alphonsi was one of those to announce her retirement. After 74 caps, a record-breaking seven consecutive Women's Six Nations Grand Slams and an 11-year international career, the inspirational openside decided it was time to make way for the next generation.

England turned to Alphonsi's Saracens team-mate and friend Hannah Gallagher to fill the number seven shirt. Some players may have balked at the prospect of replacing such a revered star, but not Gallagher, whose performances in the Women's Six Nations 2015 confirmed the Red Roses had another outstanding player in the making.

The 24-year-old was the epitome of perpetual motion during the championship – starting four of the five fixtures – and in the mould of all great openside flankers, her support play was tireless. Gallagher scored twice during the tournament and her try in the victory over Italy at the Stoop in February was outstanding. She hit the line at a devastating angle, 40 metres out, and outpaced the Azzurri full-back for an eye-catching score. Later in the game, she supplied the decisive pass for full-back Kay Wilson to score herself.

Gallagher repeated the trick in the narrow loss to France at Twickenham in March, appearing in the right place at the right time to accept a pass from prop Laura Keates and power over. Memories of Alphonsi's remarkable contribution to the England cause

for more than a decade will be not forgotten by team-mates or supporters in a hurry but, in Gallagher, the Red Roses have a player who has already significantly eased the pain of the legend's departure.

England
Rugby

IN PROFILE

Ruth Laybourn

England's most prolific finisher in this year's Women's Six Nations, flying wing Ruth Laybourn is making up for lost time on the international stage.

Position: **Wing**

Age: **30**

Height: **1.72m**

Weight: **65kg**

Caps: **10**

When she made her Test debut for the Red Roses in 2011, Laybourn marked the occasion with a hat-trick in a victory over Spain. Two more tries in her next four appearances followed, including a touchdown and a Player of the Match award in a 40-20 defeat of France at Twickenham in November 2013, and England appeared to have unearthed a new star.

Her story however took a heartbreaking twist last year when she was ruled out for nine months with a back injury. It was a bitter blow for the Darlington Mowden Park star, who also missed the Women's Rugby World Cup. But, after her enforced stint on the sidelines, Laybourn bounced back in 2015, earning a recall to the Test side and top-scoring for the Red Roses in the Women's Six Nations Championship.

Laybourn's three tries came in England's 39-7 demolition of Italy at the Twickenham Stoop in February. Her first score came after just 54 seconds , after taking a pass from Lydia Thompson and muscling her way through two tackles for the touchdown.

A fine break from Katy Mclean created the space for Laybourn's second 15 minutes into the second half, the wing taking the scoring pass from Ceri Large to score in the corner. She completed the second hat-trick of her Test career with England's sixth try, when Amber Reed moved the ball wide and a burst of pace took her past the first defender and over in the left hand corner.

Laybourn's haul of 15 points saw her finish as England's joint top scorer in the 2015 tournament, sharing the honour with Mclean. It represented a stunning return to international rugby for a player who had been cruelly denied the chance to feature at the Rugby World Cup.

No one has scored more Test points for England than record-breaking fly-half Jonny Wilkinson.

ENGLAND ALL-TIME RECORDS

From the highest points-scorer in England history to their most-capped player, the team's longest winning run in Test matches and its youngest ever captain, this section details the milestones set by those who've pulled on the famous white shirt and the record-breaking achievements of the team since the first international 144 years ago.

Appearances

THE MEN WHO HAVE SET NEW MILESTONES PLAYING FOR ENGLAND

CAPTAIN FANTASTIC

England's most capped captain is Will Carling, who led the team 59 times during his career. His first game as England captain – succeeding scrum-half Richard Harding – was against Australia, at Twickenham, in November 1988, and he last skippered the side against Ireland in March 1996. England won 44 of their 59 games with Carling as captain, claiming the 5 Nations Grand Slam in 1991, 1992 and 1995. Phil de Glanville took over, but his reign lasted eight Tests, from November 1996 to July 1997.

TEENAGE DEBUTANT

He only played 10 Tests for his country, but Colin Laird still holds the distinction as England's youngest ever player. The Harlequins fly-half was just 18 years and 124 days old when winning his first cap, against Wales at Twickenham in January 1927. He played in all four Five Nations Championship matches the following season as England completed the Grand Slam.

TWO-CAP VETERAN

The oldest man to represent England in an international is Frederick Gilbert. The full-back was 38 years and 362 days old when he made his debut, against Wales at Twickenham in 1923, and after celebrating his 39th birthday three days later, he won his second and last cap for England the following month against Ireland in Leicester.

AMATEUR PACE SETTER

The most-capped Englishman who played exclusively in the game's amateur era is Peter Winterbottom, who won 58 caps. The openside flanker made his Test debut in a 15-11 victory over Australia in 1982 and his last match was in 1993, against Ireland in Dublin, two years before the advent of professionalism. Winterbottom also played seven Tests for the British & Irish Lions and started in the Rugby World Cup 1991 final loss to the Wallabies.

Below: Flanker Joe Worsley appeared 40 times for England in the Six Nations Championship between 2000 and 2011.

SIX NATIONS STALWART

The record for the most appearances in the Six Nations Championship, since it was revamped in 2000, belongs to Joe Worsley with 40. The Wasps flanker made his debut as a replacement against Italy in Rome in the 2000, while his last appearance, also off the bench, was against Wales at the Millennium Stadium in 2011. Worsley was part of the Grand Slam winning team of 2003 and scored six Championship tries.

Above: **Ben Gollings represented England for 12 years on the Sevens World Series circuit.**

LONG-SERVING SEVENS STAR

The most experienced England player in the history of the Sevens World Series is Ben Gollings, who made 70 appearances in a 12-year Sevens career. The prolific playmaker made his tournament debut as a 19-year-old in Paris in 1999. He went on to feature in two World Cups and three Commonwealth Games, before making his final England Sevens appearance in the World Series in Edinburgh in 2011.

ENGLAND'S ONLY CENTURION

The only player to have amassed a century of caps for his country, Jason Leonard's 114 Test appearances is an England record that is yet to be eclipsed. The Harlequins prop was 22 when he made his international debut against Argentina in Buenos Aires in 1990, and played his last Test for Engalnd, 14 years later, against Italy in Rome. Leonard also holds the record for the most appearances in the Five/Six Nations, with 54, and in the Rugby World Cup – 22 games. His World Cup debut came against New Zealand at Twickenham in 1991 and he climaxed his career as a replacement against Australia in the 2003 final.

WOMEN'S RECORD BREAKER

The first England Womens player to reach the 100-cap milestone was Amy Garnett. The Saracens hooker began her international career against Spain in Barcelona in 2000 and, after featuring in three consecutive World Cup campaigns, she reached the century of Test appearances for the Red Roses in a 41-9 victory over Canada in the final of the 2011 Nations Cup. She was joined in the 100-cap club in March 2015 by Worcester prop Rochelle Clark, who reached her century against France.

UNBROKEN SEQUENCE

Will Carling also holds the record for the most consecutive England Test appearances – 44, all as captain, too – between 1989 and 1995. The centre began his remarkable run against Fiji at Twickenham in November 1989 and started in all of England's next 43 Tests, before missing out on selection for the World Cup group stage match against Italy in Durban in May 1995.

FIRST TO 50 CAPS

The modern era has seen a host of players amass 50 caps for England, but the first man to reach the milestone was Rory Underwood. The wing made his Test debut in a 12-9 victory over Ireland at Twickenham in February 1984 and, seven years later, he celebrated his 50th appearance in England's 9-6 defeat of Scotland 9-6 in the Rugby World Cup 1991 semi-final at Murrayfield.

Points

THE MEN WHO HAVE SET NEW SCORING MILESTONES PLAYING FOR ENGLAND

THE WONDER OF WILKINSON

The most prolific player in England Rugby history is Jonny Wilkinson, who scored an incredible 1,179 points in 91 Tests between 1998 and 2011. The fly-half amassed six tries, 162 conversions, 239 penalties and 36 drop goals before retiring from international rugby after the 2011 World Cup in New Zealand. His biggest individual haul in a Test was 35 points in England's 80-23 rout of Italy in the 2001 Six Nations.

SENSATIONAL IN THE 6 NATIONS

England's most prolific try-scorer exclusively in the Six Nations Championship is Ben Cohen, who scored 16 times. The Northampton wing scored two on his Championship debut against Ireland at Twickenham in 2000 and, in 29 appearances, he scored 14 more tries. Cohen's most prolific 6 Nations season was his first, with five tries in five Tests. His last RBS 6 Nations try was against France in Paris in 2004.

Right: **Wing Ben Cohen remains England's most prolific try-scorer in the 16-season history of the Six Nations Championship.**

HODGSON'S RECORD HAUL

Jonny Wilkinson's haul of 35 points against Italy, in the 2001 Six Nations, was certainly impressive, but the record for the most points by an England player in a Test match is held by Sale and Saracens fly-half Charlie Hodgson. Hodgson set the record on his Test debut against Romania at Twickenham in 2001. He scored two tries and kicked 14 conversions and two penalties for a tally of 44 points.

HAT-TRICK FIRST

The first player to score a hat-trick of Test match tries for England was Henry Taylor. The Blackheath halfback achieved it at the age of 22 in February 1881 against Ireland at Whalley Range in Manchester.

AWESOME ASHTON

Although Rory Underwood holds the record for the most career tries in the Rugby World Cup, with 11, Chris Ashton is the most prolific scorer in a single tournament, with six in New Zealand in 2011. The Saracens wing – then at Northampton – crossed twice in the group stage victory over Georgia in Dunedin before recording a hat-trick in the 67-3 win against Romania. Ashton's final try of Rugby World Cup 2011 came in the defeat of Scotland in Auckland. He is also the only England player to score four tries for England in the Six Nations Championship, achieving it against Italy in 2011 at Twickenham.

TRY SCORER SUPREME

England's most lethal finisher in Test rugby is RAF and Leicester wing Rory Underwood, who scored 49 tries in 85 internationals. His first try came in his second Test, a 32-18 defeat to France at the Parc des Princes in March 1984. His last score was in a 21-15 victory over Wales 12 years later.

LETHAL LOWE

The 1914 Championship was a good one for England as they completed the Grand Slam for the second time. It a superb season for wing Cyril Lowe, who set an England record for most tries scored in a single tournament with eight. He did not score in the opening game against Wales, but got two tries against Ireland at Twickenham and back-to-back hat-tricks against Scotland in Inverleith and France at Stade Colombes.

Above: **Chris Ashton was in sensational form for England during the 2011 Rugby World Cup in New Zealand, finishing as the joint-top try-scorer in the tournament with six.**

CHAMPIONSHIP RECORD BREAKERS

The oldest player to have scored a try for England in the RBS 6 Nations Championship (since 2000) is Nick Easter. The Harlequins number eight came off the bench against Italy, at Twickenham in February 2015, and scored the sixth try of his Test career at the age of 36 years and 183 days. The youngest man to score points for England in the Six Nations (also since 2000) is Danny Cipriani, who was aged 20 years and 139 days in 2008 when he landed a first-half penalty against Ireland at Twickenham.

GOLLINGS' POINTS DELUGE

No Englishman has played more Sevens World Series events than Ben Gollings and he is also the competition's most prolific points-scorer. He amassed a remarkable 2,652 points during his 12 years on the circuit and is also second on the all-time list of the try scorers with 220.

TOURNAMENT DOUBLE FOR JONNY

Unsurprisingly Jonny Wilkinson is the highest points scorer for England in both the Five/Six Nations Championship and the Rugby World Cup. The fly-half accumulated 546 points in Five and Six Nations games and amassed 277 points in four Rugby World Cups. Wilkinson scored 69 points in the 1999 tournament, and was even more prolific, with 113 points in Australia in 2003. The 2007 World Cup saw him score 67 points and his swansong – New Zealand in 2011 – yielded 28 points in four games.

England All-Time Team Records

THE COLLECTIVE MILESTONES SET BY ENGLAND

TRY SCORING SEQUENCE

England's longest run of consecutive Tests with at least one try is 43, set between 1911 and 1927. After drawing a blank in a 3-0 defeat to Ireland at Lansdowne Road in February 1911, England scored three tries in their next match against Scotland at Twickenham. The tries flowed for the next 16 years and this incredible sequence only ended when England lost 3-0 to France at Stade Colombes in April 1927.

SOUTHERN HEMISPHERE DOMINANCE

The scalps of the SANZAR trio of New Zealand, South Africa and Australia are prized possessions and England's longest winning sequence against the three countries collectively is 12 matches. After losing to the Springboks in the quarter-finals of Rugby World Cup 1999, England began their superb streak with a 27-22 victory over South Africa in Bloemfontein in the summer of 2000. After 11 subsequent triumphs over the three southern hemisphere heavyweights, the sequence was finally broken when the team were beaten by New Zealand in Dunedin in June 2004. The record sequence, which included successes home and away against each of the trio, featured five wins over both the Wallabies and Springboks and two over the All Blacks.

TRY BONANZA

England's record for the most tries scored in a calendar year was established in 2001 when they crossed the whitewash 70 times. The avalanche of tries came in just 11 Tests with the team scoring 10 in the 80-23 victory over Italy at Twickenham in February and a further 20 in the 134-0 demolition of Romania in November.

HOT STREAK

England's longest winning streak in Test rugby is 14 matches. The run began with a 50-10 Six Nations defeat of Wales at Twickenham in March 2002 and included wins over New Zealand, Australia and South Africa, on consecutive weekends at Twickenham in November that year, and a famous 15-13 victory over the All Blacks in Wellington in June 2003. The run came to an end when England lost 17-16 to France in a Rugby World Cup 2003 warm-up match in Marseille in August. The run saw England amass 493 points, scoring 40 or more points seven times.

Left: **Dan Luger scored two tries England's 50–10 defeat of Wales at Twickenham in March 2002, the start of their record run of 14 consecutive victories.**

ON THE ROAD

England's most successful period in terms of away Test match wins was between 2003 and 2004 when they won nine consecutive internationals on foreign soil. Rugby World Cup 2003 played a large part in the sequence, starting with the 84-6 triumph over Georgia in Perth – England's Rugby World Cup 2003 opener– and after victories over South Africa, Samoa, Uruguay, Wales, France and Australia in the final, the run stood at seven games. England extended the streak to nine with wins over Italy in Rome and Scotland at Murrayfield in the 2004 RBS 6 Nations Championship before France beat them in Paris in March.

NO PLACE LIKE HOME

Twickenham is frequently referred to as a fortress and between 1999 and 2004 is certainly lived up to its reputation as England went 22 games unbeaten at home. The phenomenal run began with a 101-10 rout of Tonga in the group stages of the World Cup and included a hat-trick of wins over both the Wallabies and the Springboks as well as a 31-28 victory over the All Blacks. The sequence included 113 tries and 1024 points in total and was finally brought to an end in March 2004 after a 19-13 loss to Ireland, England's first defeat as the reigning world champions.

Left: **Austin Healey dives over the line to score one of England's 13 tries in their 101–10 defeat of Tonga in the Rugby World Cup of 1999, which started the 22–Test unbeaten run.**

MISERLY DEFENCE

Preventing the opposition from scoring a single point is a rarity in Test rugby, but England have twice achieved it three matches in succession. Their first triple clean sheet was achieved in 1892 in the Home Nations Championship, when they overcame Wales 17-0 in Blackheath, Ireland 7-0 in Manchester and Scotland 5-0 in Edinburgh. England repeated the feat, 70 years later, in three consecutive Tests at Twickenham, beating Scotland 6-0 in March 1961, drawing 0-0 with Wales in January 1962 before defeating Ireland 16-0 the following month.

FAVOURITE OPPONENTS

Although England have faced Scotland more times than any other nation in their Test history, they have recorded the most wins over Ireland. The first Anglo-Irish game was staged at the Kennington Oval in 1875. In the 129 games between the two nations, in all competitions up to the end of the RBS 6 Nations 2015, England had won 74 times. Ireland is also England's favourite country away from home with the 32 wins in 66 visits.

TWICKENHAM LANDSLIDE

The biggest win in the England Test history is the 134-0 victory over Romania at Twickenham in November 2001. The one-sided rout at HQ featured 20 tries with Jason Robinson scoring four and Ben Cohen and Dan Luger both registering hat-tricks while Charlie Hodgson added two more tries and landed 14 conversions and two penalties.

HISTORIC HIGHLIGHT

England's most successful winning sequence in the amateur era came in the 19th century when they won 10 consecutive games. The run began with a victory over Wales in Swansea in December 1882 and, after nine more triumphs, it ended when England were held to a draw by Scotland in Edinburgh in March 1886.

A YEAR TO REMEMBER

The finest calendar year for the England in terms of victories was 2003 when Clive Woodward's won 16 Tests in 17 matches. They claimed the scalps of New Zealand, South Africa and Australia in the year in which they lifted the World Cup and the only blemish on their otherwise faultless record was a narrow 17-16 loss to France in Marseille in August in a friendly. It was also a record-breaking 12 months in terms of points scored with the side amassing 644, an average of almost 38 points per Test.

WOODWARD'S DEFENCE

The RBS 6 Nations Championship 2003 saw Clive Woodward's side achieve the Grand Slam. It was also the campaign in which England conceded the fewest points in a Six Nations season. They conceded just four tries and 46 points in five matches. France were the only side to record double figures against England, losing 25-17 at Twickenham.

ROUT IN ROME

While the 111-13 romp against Uruguay at Rugby World Cup 2003 was England's biggest ever victory away from home, Brisbane was a neutral venue. The team's biggest win in a fixture on at opponent's home came against Italy in the inaugural Six Nations Championship in 2000. England ran in eight tries at the Stadio Flaminio in Rome, including a hat-trick from Austin Healy, as they ran out 59-12 winners.

ALL SQUARE

Up to the end of the 2015 RBS 6 Nations, England had been involved in 50 draws in 685 Tests. A record 18 of those stalemates have come against Scotland with the first match between the two teams to finish level coming in Glasgow in 1873. The most recent draw was the 15-15 final score in the RBS 6 Nations Championship at Murrayfield in 2010.

Right: **Fly–half Toby Flood, who landed two penalties in England's 15-15 draw with Scotland at Murrayfield in 2010, just about gets this clearance kick away.**

CHAMPIONSHIP STREAK

England's record for most consecutive wins in the Home/Five/Six Nations Championship is 10, in the 1920s. The sequence began in the final match of the 1922 Five Nations, when England beat Scotland 11-5 at Twickenham. Back-to-back Grand Slams in 1923 and 1924 extended the winning run to nine and it reached double figures when Wavell Wakefield's team despatched Wales 12-6 at Twickenham in the opening game of the 1925 Championship. The run ended with a 6-6 draw against Ireland, also at Twickenham, in February 1925

FAVOURITE FOE

In terms of winning percentage, Italy are England's opposition of choice with 21 victories in the 21 meetings between the two teams. The Red Rose first played the Azzurri at Twickenham in the World Cup in October 1991, winning 36-6 courtesy of a brace of tries from Jeremy Guscott, while their most recent triumph was their 47-17 success at Twickenham in the RBS 6 Nations Championship 2015, built on two tries from centre Jonathan Joseph.

CENTURY MILESTONES

England have surpassed the 100-point mark five times in Test matches. The 110-0 rout of the Netherlands in 1998 was their first international century and they achieved it twice against the USA and Tonga the following year. Romania were despatched 134-0 in 2001 while England's most recent three-figure score was in 2003 as Uruguay were demolished 111-13 in Rugby World Cup 2003 in Australia. success at Twickenham in the RBS 6 Nations Championship 2015, built on two tries from centre Jonathan Joseph.

Below: **Jonathan Joseph crossed twice in England's 47–17 victory over Italy at Twickenham in 2015.**

Other All-Time England Records

THE MEN AND MATCHES TO HAVE MADE ENGLAND RUGBY HISTORY

QUICK-FIRE PRICE

England's fastest ever try was scored by Leo Price in a Five Nations Championship match against Wales at Twickenham in 1923. The flanker touched down after just 10 seconds and the team went on to win the match 7-3.

Below: **Jonny Wilkinson was recognised as the game's greatest player after England's Rugby World Cup triumph.**

RANKINGS FIRST

England hold the distinction as the only team from the northern hemisphere to have been ranked the number one side in the world. First published in April 2003, England topped the inaugural World Rugby Rankings and they held top spot until being deposed by New Zealand in June 2004.

WILKINSON ACCOLADE

England's all-time leading points scorer, Jonny Wilkinson also holds the distinction as the only Englishman to have been named the World Rugby Player of the Year. First awarded in 2001, the accolade was given to Wilkinson two years later after the fly-half was instrumental in England's victory over the Wallabies in the final of the World Cup. The prolific number 10 averaged nearly 17 points per match in 2003 and the Red Rose won all 13 Tests he played during the year. England players Jason Robinson (2002), Steve Thompson (2003), Tom Croft (2009) and Owen Farrell (2012) have also been shortlisted for the award.

DAZZLING DEBUT

Fred Chapman has the honour of scoring the fastest try in his England debut. A wing for the Westoe club, Chapman debuted against Wales at Twickenham in 1910 and scored in the corner after 75 seconds. It was also the first ever international try scored at Twickenham.

NUMBERS GAME

England played the first ever Test match to feature players wearing numbered shirts. The game took place in Cardiff against Wales in January 1922 and saw the home side emerge 28-6 winners.

DROP GOAL DISTINCTION

Flanker Neil Back holds an unusual record – he is the only England forward to have landed a drop goal in a Test match. He did it in England's 59-12 victory over Italy in Rome in 2000.

SHORT BUT SWEET

The briefest England career on record in terms of minutes on the pitch was that of Nick Walshe. The scrum-half actually won two caps on England's 2006 tour of Australia, but he saw just five minutes of action in those two Tests.

OFF THE BENCH

The first man to make an appearance for England as a Test match replacement was Coventry's Timothy Dalton. The wing came off the bench to replace the injured Keith Fielding against Scotland at Twickenham in March 1969. It was Dalton's only England appearance.

ASHTON'S AMAZING YEAR

The record for the most tries in a calendar year belongs to Chris Ashton. The wing was still a Northampton Saint in 2011 when he touched down 12 times in 11 Tests.. His impressive haul included four tries against Italy at Twickenham in the RBS 6 Nations Championship and a hat-trick against Romania in Dunedin at the Rugby World Cup. The record for most points in a year belongs to Jonny Wilkinson with 233 in 14 Tests in 2003.

SYDNEY MILESTONE

The highest attendance for an England international was recorded on 22 November 2003 when 82,957 fans descended on Stadium Australia in Sydney to witness the dramatic extra-time victory over the Wallabies in the Rugby World Cup final. The record crowd for a game at Twickenham was set in November 2014 when 82,223 fans were on hand to watch England play the All Blacks.

Below: **A record crowd of 82,957 watched England defeat Australia in the 2003 Rugby World Cup final.**

Above: **John Bentley appeared in four Tests for England during his cross-code career.**

PERFECT RECORD

Up to the end of the 2015 RBS 6 Nations Championship, England had played Test matches against 19 countries in their 144-year history. They boast an unbeaten record against 11 opponents: Romania, Japan, United States, Fiji, Italy, Canada, Samoa, the Netherlands, Tonga, Georgia and Uruguay.

CODE BREAKER

The advent of professionalism in 1995 allowed rugby league players to switch codes and the first player to play for England following the move was John Bentley. The wing had already won two caps for England in 1988 before turning professional and returned to the England side in July 1997 when he selected against Australia in Sydney.

UNDERWOOD'S HOT STREAK

England's all-time leading try scorer, Rory Underwood also holds the record for scoring in most consecutive Tests. The RAF and Leicester wing began his superb six-match sequence with two tries against Ireland at Twickenham in March 1988 and in his next appearance the following month he scored against Ireland in Dublin. Tries in both Tests against Australia in the summer followed before he registered doubles against Fiji in Suva and the Wallabies, again, at Twickenham at the end of the year.

FRESH-FACED CAPTAIN

England's match against Scotland at Raeburn Place, Edinburgh, in March 1871 was rugby's first ever Test, and it also witnessed the youngest ever player to captain the team. The skipper was Blackheath forward Frederic Stokes, who was just 20 years and 258 days old, when he led out the team. Stokes played two more Tests for England, captaining the side on both occasions. The oldest man to captain England is Sale hooker Eric Evans, who was 37 years and 42 days old when leading the team against Scotland at Murrayfield in 1958. It was his 30th and final appearance for England.

COMEBACK KINGS

England's Test match against Australia, at Twickenham in November 2002, has the record for the biggest deficit overhauled by the team. They were trailing the Wallabies by 12 points in the 56th minute, but a storming final quarter saw England snatch a dramatic 32-31 win.

Left: Scrum-half Matt Dawson leads a break during England's 32–31 victory over Australia at Twickenham in 2002, when the men in white overturned a record 12-point deficit.

GRAND SLAM QUADRUPLE

Four England players have won the Championship Grand Slam four times in their career. The first to achieve the feat were fly-half William Davies and wing Cyril Lowe, who were both part of the team in 1913, 1914, 1921 and 1923. Second row Ron Cove-Smith played in the last two of those campaigns and was also involved in the Grand Slam seasons of 1924 and 1928. The most recent member of the club is Jason Leonard who played in 1991, 1992, 1995 and 2003, the last of which was the only one in the Six Nations Championship era.

SWEEPING CHANGES

The England team named to face Wales in a Rugby World Cup 2003 warm-up match in Cardiff made history, as it was the first time the starting XV had been completely different from the one that had played the previous Test. England's last game had been against Australia in June but not one of the team who started in Melbourne were in the XV to start against Wales two months later.

PROFESSIONAL FIRST

The first player to make his Test debut in the professional era was Mark Regan. The Bath and Bristol hooker won his first of his 47 caps, 1995–2008, against South Africa at Twickenham in November 1995 – England's first match following the historic change in the game's rules.

RAPID CENTURION

The first player to register 100 points for England was Harlequins full-back Bob Hiller, who reached the milestone in his 14th Test appearance, scoring all his side's 14 points in a 14-14 draw with France at Twickenham in February 1971. The quickest player to post the century for England is fly-half Paul Grayson, his 21 points at Twickenham against Scotland in 1997. The milestone was reached in only his sixth Test.

KEEPING IT IN THE FAMILY

There have been 13 father and son combinations to represent England at Test level. The first family to achieve the feat was the Miltons – father William won two caps in 1874 and 1875, while his sons John and Cecil both represented England in the 1900s. Since then the Birkett (Reginald and John), Tucker (William and Bill), Wilkinson (Harry J. and Harry), Hubbard (George and John), Hobbs (Reginald F.A. and Reginald G.S.), Weston (Henry and William), Scott (Frank and Edward), Preece (Ivor and Peter), Greenwood (Dick and Will), Fidler (John and Rob) and Youngs (Nick, Ben and Tom) families have all emulated the feat. The most recent family to boast two generations of England players are the Farrells, son Owen making his Test debut against Scotland in 2012, five years after father Andy's last appearance for England.

England Rugby
Rugby

England Rugby FanZone

Rugby World Cup 2015 promises to be the most interactive tournament yet and England supporters can keep up to date with all the news about the men in white from Stuart Lancaster and his squad in even more ways than ever.

As the sense of anticipation builds across the country ahead of the kick-off of this year's festival of rugby, England fans will never be far from the heart of the action as their heroes bid to lift the Webb Ellis Cup on home soil.

They can sign up to either the England Rugby Supporters Club and with membership they will get access to a wide range of exciting and exclusive benefits, including priority access to tickets, special discounts on travel, merchandise and stadium tours. Members get all the news from the England camps first, while in the FanZone, there will be exclusive wallpapers, the England Rugby screensaver, England Rugby Ezines and videos of the England Rugby team.

For younger fans, the Junior Supporters Club offers loads of fun and interesting things to do. Members can find out all the latest gossip from within the England camp, learn tips and skills from their rugby heroes, and have the chance to walk out of the Twickenham tunnel with the England team as a mascot.

Registering as an official England Rugby Supporters Club member, however, is just the start of the Rugby Football Union's growing conversation with fans who can also make sure they are part of it through a variety of social media.

The England Rugby Facebook page is rapidly approaching the one-a-half-million Likes milestone and is a great place for video highlights, match reports and news updates from Twickenham. The RFU's Twitter account – @EnglandRugby – has almost 400,000 followers and offers the chance to interact with other supporters.

The Official RFU iPhone app, sponsored by O2, is the best way to stay in touch with England Rugby on the move, from grassroots to the England Team, and it offers live news and real-time England match commentary, plus the knowledge to settle pub arguments with instantly updated team line-ups and match statistics.

In the FanZone section, supporters can find their way around the seats, pubs, bars and landmarks of Twickenham Stadium and the surrounding area. There are quick links to buy tickets online – with access to O2 Priority tickets for O2 customers – and other exclusive offers from RFU sponsors.

For younger fans, there's the "Ruckley's Tryfest" app, featuring England Rugby's bulldog mascot and launched in February this year, an action-packed, high-speed game of skill and strategy using touchscreen technology which encourages players to think strategically in selecting and placing characters, learning to identify and use their special abilities to achieve victory in 40 levels.

"Ruckley's Tryfest is an exciting initiative that brings rugby on to a new platform and allows us to increase engagement with fans in a new way," said Laura Marchant, the RFU's Brand Manager. "Ruckley embodies the RFU's core values and these are importantly reflected throughout the game. Ruckley has made a big impact since joining England Rugby in 2013 and we are delighted to be building on this success for the benefit of our fans."

The official England Rugby YouTube channel features a host of exclusive videos including training sessions, interviews, Try of the Month highlights and even the story of how "Swing Low, Sweet Chariot" became the anthem of the national team.

Right: **Ruckley is the mascot of the England Rugby team**

The England Rugby Quiz

How much do you know about England Rugby? Here are 50 questions on a variety of topics, the answers to almost all of which can be found somewhere in this book.

THE PLAYERS

1. How many tries did Rory Underwood score for England in his record-breaking international career?
2. Against which team did Jason Leonard win his milestone 100th cap in 2003?
3. Johnny Wilkinson is the most prolific player in the history of England Rugby, but who is second on the all-time Test points list with 400?
4. How many times did Will Carling captain England in his international career?
5. How many caps had Chris Robshaw won before Stuart Lancaster appointed him as England captain for the RBS 6 Nations game against Scotland in February 2012?
6. When Rochelle Clark won her 100th cap against France in March 2015, she joined which other England woman on a century of international appearances?
7. Which player holds the record for the longest England career in terms of years between Test debut and final cap?
8. Which player holds the record for the most appearances for England in Sevens World Series rugby?
9. Jonny Wilkinson won the World Rugby Player of the Year accolade in 2003, but which other England player was also shortlisted for that year's award?
10. Who was the first rugby league convert to earn an England Test cap in the professional era?

THE TEAM

1. England men's record run of consecutive Test victories (March 2002–August 2003) comprised how many matches?
2. How many Women's Six Nations matches did England lose during their run of seven consecutive Championships, 2006–12?
3. In which year did England finally beat South Africa (the last of the southern hemisphere "big three") for the first time?
4. England's record for most tries in a Test came against Romania in 2001, but how many times did they touch down?
5. Against which Test nation have England recorded the most victories?
6. England's first Test against southern hemisphere opposition was against New Zealand in 1905, but where was the match played?
7. How many tries have England scored in all their Test matches, 1871–2015?
8. How many of England's 685 Test matches have ended in a draw?
9. Excluding New Zealand Natives in 1889 and Presidents XV in 1971, against how many different opponents have England played Test matches, 1871–2015?
10. Who is the longest-serving England head coach?

THE RUGBY WORLD CUP

1. Who, 1987, were England's first-ever Rugby World Cup opponents?
2. Who was England's captain during Rugby World Cup 2007 in France?
3. Who was England's top scorer in Rugby World Cup 1991, when they were last hosts?
4. England opened their Rugby World Cup 2003 campaign with an 84-6 victory over which country in the pool stage?

5 Who was England's top points-scorer at Women's Rugby World Cup 2014 in France?

6 Who was England head coach at Rugby World Cup 2007 when they reached their third final?

7 Which Englishman was the joint top try scorer with France's Vincent Clerc at Rugby World Cup 2011?

8 Who scored England's first-ever try in the Rugby World Cup?

9 When did England – Women's Rugby World Cup 2014 champions – first win this competition?

10 How many times have England met Australia (Pool A opponents in 2015) in previous Rugby World Cups?

FIVE/SIX NATIONS CHAMPIONSHIP

1 England have won more Five/Six Nations Championships Grand Slams than any other country, but how many have they recorded?

2 How many tries have England scored in the history of the Six Nations Championship, 2000–15 (it is the record total)?

3 Who made the most appearances for England in the Six Nations Championship?

4 In which year did England set the record for the most points scored in a single Five/Six Nations Championship season?

5 Who scored England's first every try in the Six Nations Championship?

6 Who has made the most Five/Six Nations Championship appearances for England?

7 England's record for the most penalties kicked in a Championship campaign is 18, held jointly by Jonny Wilkinson and which other player?

8 When wing Cyril Lowe set England's record for most tries in a single Five Nations Championship season in 1914, how many did he score?

9 Jason Robinson and which other player scored a team-leading three tries for England in 2003, the last time they won the RBS 6 Nations Grand Slam?

10 Up to end of the 2015 RBS 6 Nations, England had played 191 Championship fixtures at Twickenham. How many victories at HQ had they registered?

TWICKENHAM

1 When England played their first-ever Test match at Twickenham in 1910, who were their opponents?

2 England's record undefeated run at Twickenham lasted from 1999 to 2004, but which country ended that streak?

3 Which was the first country, in 1913, ever to defeat England at Twickenham?

4 How many matches will Twickenham stage during the 2015 Rugby World Cup?

5 How many Twickenham Test matches have been cancelled due to bad weather?

6 What was the attendance when England faced Australia in the Rugby World Cup 1991 final?

7 How long is the Twickenham pitch?

8 Which famous annual fixture was first played at Twickenham in 1921?

9 Twickenham has the fourth largest capacity of any European sports stadium; which three have more?

10 How many times did Twickenham host the Heineken Cup final between 1995 and 2014?

Answers

Players: 1. 49. 2. France. 3. Paul Grayson. 4. 59. 5. One. 6. Amy Garnett. 7. Simon Shaw (1996-2011). 8. Ben Gollings (70 appearances). 9. Steve Thompson. 10. John Bentley (vs Australia, 1997).
The Team: 1. 14. 2. One (16-15 to Wales in 2009). 3. South Africa (11-8). 4. 20 (Jason Robinson 4, Ben Cohen 3, Dan Luger 3, Charlie Hodgson 4, Lewis Moody 2, Mike Tindall 2, Austin Healey, Mark Regan, Alex Sanderson, Joe Worsley). 5. Ireland (74). 6. Crystal Palace. 7. 2,486. 8. 50. 9. 20 (Scotland, Ireland).

Rugby World Cup: 1. Australia (lost 19-6). 2. Phil Vickery. 3. Jonathan Webb (56 points). 4. Georgia. 5. Emily Scarratt (70 points). 6. Brian Ashton. 7. Chris Ashton (five). 8. Mike Harrison (vs Australia, 1987). 9. 1994. 10. Five.

Wales, France, Italy, New Zealand, South Africa, Australia, Argentina, Romania, Japan, United States, Fiji, Canada, Samoa, Netherlands, Tonga, Georgia, Uruguay, Pacific Islanders). 10. Sir Clive Woodward (November 1997-September 2004).

Five/Six Nations Championship: 1. 12. 2. 232. 3. Joe Worsley (40). 4. 2001. 5. Ben Cohen (vs Ireland, February 2000). 6. Jason Leonard (54 matches). 7. 125 metres. 8. The Varsity Match. 9. Will Greenwood. 10. 130.

Twickenham: 1. Wales. 2. 22. 3. South Africa. 4. Ten. 5. 2 (1947, vs France, and 1987, vs Scotland). 6. 56,208. 7. The Varsity Match, 8. Nou Camp (Barcelona), Wembley, Croke Park (Dublin). 10. Four (2000, 2004, 2007, 2012).

Credits

The publishers would like to thank the following sources for their kind permission to reproduce the pictures in this book.

ACTION IMAGES: /Henry Browne: 75R; /Jed Leicester: 136-137
ALAMY: /Action Plus Sports Images: 110-111
HUW EVANS PICTURE AGENCY: 127
CHRIS FARROW: 124, 125
GETTY IMAGES: 42, 120, 121, 123; /Allsport: 51R; /Steve Bardens/The RFU Collection: 18, 27; /Shaun Botterill: 52R, 147; /Paolo Bruno: 68; /Jon Buckle: 153; /David Cannon: 10-11, 32C, 148; /Russell Cheyne: 53R; /Harry Engels: 70-71, 74, 76, 77L, 77R, 140; /Julian Finney: 19, 21; /Stu Forster: 72-73, 75L, 90; /Gallo Images: 65; /Paul Gilham: 87; /Cate Gillon: 47B; /Laurence Griffiths: 12-13, 28T, 58, 59, 130-131; /Richard Heathcote: 151, 160; /Mike Hewitt: 40, 44, 54, 84, 85, 92-93, 141, 157; /Ken Ishii: 105; /Ross Kinnaird: 149; /Jan Kruger: 96, 99, 101; /Warren Little: 56, 113, 114; /Jordan Mansfield: 89; /Tony Marshall/The RFU Collection: 102-103, 106, 109; /Clive Mason: 16, 146; /Ethan Miller: 145; /Jeff J Mitchell: 64, 150; /Dan Mullan: 97, 98; /Ignacio Naon: 62; /Adam Pretty: 55L; /Vaughn Ridley: 45; /Nigel Roddis: 43, 80, 81T, 81C; /David Rogers: 4-5, 22, 23, 24, 25, 39, 50, 51L, 52L, 53L, 57, 60, 128-129, 152, 154; /David Rogers/The RFU Collection: 7, 9, 14, 15L, 15R, 20, 30, 31, 34, 35, 37, 41, 55R, 82L, 83, 132, 133, 134, 135; /Miguel Rojo/AFP: 63; /Clive Rose: 26, 28B; /Tom Shaw: 144; /Tom Shaw/The RFU Collection: 94-95; /Cameron Spencer: 66, 67, 104; /Michael Steele: 32T, 61, 69, 82R; /Mark Thompson: 155; /Ullstein Bild: 116; /Phil Walter: 142-143; /Ian Walton: 47T
HASBEANZ.COM: /Neil Kennedy: 115
INPHO PHOTOGRAPHY: /James Crombie: 118-119; /Dan Sheridan: 79B
RUGBY FOOTBALL UNION: 49
RUGBYMATTERS: 91, 138, 139
SHUTTERSTOCK: 117
SPORTSFILE: /Piaras Ó Mídheach: 78, 79T

Every effort has been made to acknowledge correctly and contact the source and/or copyright holder of each picture and Carlton Books Limited apologises for any unintentional errors or omissions, which will be, corrected in future editions of this book.